Praise for *Rippling*

"With *Rippling*, Beverly Schwartz has advanced thinking and practice about entrepreneurial endeavours that strive to transform systems. Her key contribution lies in the practical aspects of becoming a changemaker, whether or not one sets out to start one's own venture or join the growing ecosystem of organizations springing up around the world to support these pragmatic visionaries and their teams."

—**Pamela Hartigan,** director, Skoll Centre for Social Entrepreneurship, Said Business School, University of Oxford, and cofounder, Volans

"From toilets for slums to technology linking small-scale farmers with international markets, *Rippling* takes readers on an inspiring journey to places where smart ideas and innovative business models are tackling big global problems. This is an important and timely book for anyone interested in new solutions for our complex and fast-changing world."

—**Sarah Murray,** *Financial Times* contributor

"Packed with examples of changemakers tackling the world's thorniest challenges, *Rippling* is a must-read for anyone committed to effecting positive change, regardless of age, income, or geography. Schwartz inspires with her blueprint for committed social entrepreneurs to fundamentally change the very systems that those less creative simply assume are so."

—**Terry Babcock-Lumish,** Newman director of public policy and distinguished lecturer, Roosevelt House Public Policy Institute, and founder, Islay Consulting LLC

"While conflict and disharmony dominate the news, *Rippling* reminds us of the tremendous good that individuals are doing all around the globe. It is truly inspirational for anyone wanting to be a changemaker."

—**Rob Donovan,** professor of behavioural research, Centre for Behavioural Research in Cancer Control, Curtin University, Australia

RIPPLING

HOW SOCIAL ENTREPRENEURS
SPREAD INNOVATION THROUGHOUT
THE WORLD

Beverly Schwartz

Foreword by Bill Drayton

JOSSEY-BASS
A Wiley Imprint
www.josseybass.com

Published by Jossey-Bass
A Wiley Imprint
One Montgomery Street, Suite 1200, San Francisco, CA 94104-4594
www.josseybass.com

Jossey-Bass books and products are available through most bookstores. To contact Jossey-Bass directly call our Customer Care Department within the U.S. at 800-956-7739, outside the U.S. at 317-572-3986, or fax 317-572-4002.

Wiley publishes in a variety of print and electronic formats and by print-on-demand. Some material included with standard print versions of this book may not be included in e-books or in print-on-demand. If this book refers to media such as a CD or DVD that is not included in the version you purchased, you may download this material at http://booksupport.wiley.com. For more information about Wiley products, visit www.wiley.com.

Library of Congress Cataloging-in-Publication Data

Schwartz, Beverly.
  Rippling : how social entrepreneurs spread innovation throughout the world / Beverly Schwartz ; foreword by Bill Drayton.—1st ed.
    p. cm.
  Includes bibliographical references and index.
  ISBN 978-1-118-13859-5 (cloth) ISBN 978-1-118-22543-1 (ebk);
ISBN 978-1-118-23883-7 (ebk); ISBN 978-1-118-26352-5 (ebk)
  1. Social entrepreneurship. 2. Social change. I. Title.
  HD60.S389 2012
  338'.04—dc23
                                                                2011052645

Printed in the United States of America
FIRST EDITION
HB Printing   10 9 8 7 6 5 4 3 2 1

To my father—whose faith in me gave me faith in myself.

To the greater good in the world—where changemakers, at all levels, really do exist . . . everywhere.

CONTENTS

PART FIVE

Cultivating Empathy   200
Reflections by Arianna Huffington

FOREWORD

Are You Ready for The Big One?

THERE ARE SMALL AND BIG CHANGES. AND THEN, VERY RARELY, THERE comes a tectonic shift so profound that everything is transformed in a historical instant.

Such transformations are as powerful as they are because they change the structure of how humans work together. A big advance of this type indeed changes everything—including the skills everyone must master, how groups and society organize, and how we all see the world. Technological revolutions, for example those in electronics or chemistry, do not begin to compare. The closest historical analogue is the agricultural revolution.

Today, after three centuries of tectonic acceleration, we are, I believe, already in the transformation zone of as big a shift as we have ever seen. The rate of change is accelerating exponentially. So is the growth in the number and the skills of the people actively causing change, and the connections between them.

It is clear where we are headed.

In a world where everything changes, and where every change bumps many other elements, causing them to change, the old social system is fast failing. Organizations in which a few people direct everyone else may have worked when the group and its members learned a skill and performed repetitive tasks year after year. This world of invisible peasantry, the Henry Ford assembly line, and the law firm increasingly will not be able to cope.

What is needed to contribute value—and to be able to compete and survive—is instead a fluid, quick, and often changing team of teams. The growth of the Web reflects and serves this accelerating need for flexible, kaleidoscopic global collaboration. When a new opportunity to contribute to a valuable change arises, successful groups will pull together teams and alliances of teams, from wherever they are, to bring together the right contribution of vision and experience and skills. And those teams of teams will keep changing as the change they serve evolves.

But a team can only be a team if everyone on it is a player.

And, in a world increasingly defined by change, being a player increasingly means one must be able to imagine and contribute to change. There will still be repetitive tasks. We will still have to wash the dishes. But anyone who is not a changemaker will be able to contribute little.

We can get a glimpse of this new world by looking at the islands of collaborating changemakers that already exist, for example, in the fluid interchanges of Silicon Valley (consider the free movement of people, the increase in open-sourcing, and the Valley's rapidly evolving support structures) or the Ashoka community of leading social and allied business entrepreneurs (consider its breakthrough beyond solo entrepreneuring to "collaborative entrepreneurship" and www.changemakers.com). These early islands are learning and evolving fast and increasingly relying on alliances and teamwork.

We already see the old systems failing all around us. Threatened people reverting to backward-looking fundamentalism. Old institutions unable to deal with the new reality—both internally or in terms of their roles.

What is needed now more than anything else is for society to go through what Ashoka calls "the awareness tipping zone" very, very soon. In all major changes, awareness is the trigger that leads to action. Once many people see the change that is coming, and what it means for them, they begin to act. And when they see one another acting, it makes conversation and action safer and increasingly unavoidable.

The media then jumps in as the contagion spreads and more and more people want to know what is happening and, in fact, urgently need a map. For example, in the American press, mentions of civil rights increased 300 percent in the 1950s and 600 percent in the first half of the 1960s as everyone focused on, talked about, and then changed how they thought and acted. Once the country had done so, its need for daily stories, the vehicle through which most learning takes place, fell sharply—with the result that media coverage declined as quickly as it earlier had grown.

The "everyone a changemaker"™ age that is now upon us will change your life and those around you profoundly. Are you ready? Will you be able to help lead the transformation?

- If you love a six-year-old, will you help her master the complex, challenging, learned skill of empathy? To the degree she does not, she will be unable to go on to the other essential skills those involved in change must have—teamwork, leadership, and changemaking—and she risks being marginalized.
- Are you ready to help the teens in your life master the above four skills by helping them practice being changemakers now?
- Are you prepared to help the institutions about which you care see the challenge and become "everyone a changemaker" organizations able to survive and flourish?
- Will you help lead society through this historic moment?

As Darwin's work in the mid-1800s makes clear, it is not the strongest species that survive, nor the most intelligent, but the ones most adaptable when faced with change.

All these questions point to why this book should be valuable to you.

Social entrepreneurs are critical to this transformation. Changing the world's systems is what defines entrepreneurship. Doing so for the good of all, which is absolutely essential now, is what defines social entrepreneurs. That is why the field has grown so very rapidly over the last thirty years. (When Ashoka was formally launched in 1980, there was not even a word to describe the field.)

This volume will introduce you to a rich sampling of the world's leading social entrepreneurs. You will quickly intuit what defines them, which should help you sense if this is a path you might take as well.

You will also get a feel for where change is headed in each field and overall. This will help you map the directions you and those around you should be considering.

You have a great guide for this journey. Bev Schwartz has been a colleague at Ashoka for seven years now. Earlier she was one of the leaders of the emerging fields of social marketing, smoking prevention, and HIV/AIDS awareness. Perhaps most important, she has long been committed to the good of all.

January 2012   Bill Drayton
                                                                        Ashoka

PROLOGUE

One should not search for an abstract meaning of life. Everyone has his own specific vocation or mission in life to carry out a concrete assignment which demands fulfillment. Therein he cannot be replaced, nor can his life be repeated. Thus, everyone's task is as unique as is his specific opportunity to implement it.

—VIKTOR FRANKL, *Man's Search for Meaning*

THREE THOUGHTS CROSSED MY MIND WHEN I FIRST STARTED TO think about writing this book. One was *I wish I had had the courage to have done this earlier in life.* That thought opened up a line of introspection that led to my second thought: *Would I be able to do justice to the innovation, the ingenuity, the bravery of the people I chose to represent the five approaches to system change that I discuss within?* And that brought me to my third thought, contemplating the concept of the word *insecurity* and its ugly stepsister, *embarrassment.* How many times have I stopped short of doing something that would have changed my life due to them? Embarrassment as a behavioral modifier may have some redeeming value—but honestly, ask yourself, how many things have you *not* done in your life because of your fear of embarrassment, or because your deep-seated insecurities about the limits of your capabilities diminished your desire to take a risk? The dictionary defines *risk* as a situation involving exposure to danger or the possibility that something unpleasant or unwelcome will happen. So where is the (your) danger? What will turn out badly (for you) and who is really being threatened by what?

If insecurity and embarrassment are socially learned behaviors, what part of them can we unlearn? Can we grow out of them, consciously or unconsciously? What part of each is missing in someone who steps out of line to follow their passion and more completely blend it into their daily life? Why do some people take personal and professional risks and place themselves in alternative realities rather consistently, and others do it so rarely?

I was thinking about that question one day when I visited an exhibit of Norman Rockwell paintings at the National Museum of Art in Washington D.C. I stopped in front of "Boy on a High Dive," which as the title states portrays a boy crouched at the edge of a diving board high in the sky looking into what seems to be a rather far-away swimming pool.[1] What a metaphor for life! The painting brought back memories of the absolute fear I had as I had stood on what felt like that same board in the same place looking into that same swimming pool many times before in my own life. Haven't we all, at one time or another, been faced with the challenge of a new and untested action? Aren't we all standing there on the high board at some time in our life contemplating taking a plunge that others may not? I believe that anyone reading this will remember and understand the exact moment that I am describing.

I've often thought about all the things I could have done and how my path would have been different if I had jumped off the board a little sooner and even more frequently. Maybe traveled down one of Robert Frost's roads not taken. I, perhaps like you, have certainly not lived without acting in socially conscious ways—but unlike the social entrepreneurs profiled in this book, I have not given up my life as I knew it after witnessing or being part of an injustice that cried out for a solution. I have come to realize that maybe, like Frankl, my own "mission in life and concrete assignment that demands fulfillment" is to make people aware that jumping into a pool of social solutions and rippling contributions along to others is deeply fulfilling. And it is astonishingly significant to all who want to shape the world into the place where we can successfully, happily, and fairly coexist with others.

The idea for this book began with the feeling of awe and amazement that I felt for the overwhelming majority of Ashoka Fellows I have met over the years. But even then, I was caught off guard by the sheer sense of joy and unbridled incredulity that enveloped me in the middle of each interview I conducted. I walked away almost floating on air. With the conclusion of every interview, I became more optimistic about people, society, the future. And I became more and more determined to jump off my high board and write this book. The examples I profile reconnected me with the words of Buddha: "An idea that is developed and put into action is more important than an idea that exists only as an idea." This book is my idea put into action. It is my Nietzsche's "why," my Frankl's "opportunity to implement," my Frost's road not taken. It is another of my social dreams that I will wait no longer to act upon. While you read this, I invite you to jump off the high board with me.

In its first run printing, *Rippling* became available in North America during the springtime. This was not a coincidence but a determination to have the book read at the time of the year most associated with the cycle of renewal and new growth. New life cyclically unfolds in spring, from tree branches budding to flowers opening to the warmth of the sun. So too it is a time for humankind to expand and flourish and open to a new cycle of growth that has laid dormant in our souls.

We are, now more than ever, all part of an ever-evolving cycle of change. Each one of us already committed to taking social actions, and those who are closer to doing so, have a rather spectacular and important role to play in creating a world of justice, equality, peace, and prosperity, while spreading happiness, hope, and inspiration to millions of people around the world. We face no shortage of opportunities, only a shortage of bold actions.

I am a huge proponent of engaged and participatory learning. Conversely, life has so often taught us, there is a time to give and a time to receive. So forgive me when I ask that as you read this book, you put yourself in the "receive mode." As you move through each section, get lost in it—marvel at the way society is changing—and give yourself the space to feel fully engaged, inspired, and hopeful. As you breathe this book in, make your breath the bridge between your inner self and the external world. Breathe in this book and breathe out the changemaker within your soul.

He who has a why to live for can bear almost any how.

—FRIEDRICH NIETZSCHE

INTRODUCTION

Rippling Solutions into System Change

JUST ABOUT ANYONE THE WORLD OVER WHO HAS USED A CELL PHONE or a computer, posted on Facebook, or tweeted understands exactly how fast the world is changing. The old ways of doing many things have evolved, accelerated, transformed, been reorganized and restructured. From the slums in India to the mountains of Nepal, from the farms in Kenya to the streets of New York and the pampas of Argentina—all lives have been touched in some way by recent rapid technologic and electronic advances. Simultaneously, consecutively, and consequently "the times they are a-changing," and in a large part of the world, the way we are now all living our lives is way different from what it was even five or ten years ago. Along with these changes we see progress—economically, politically, and socially. But at the same time, rapid growth puts stress on other overlapping systems, and though progress does mitigate a myriad of social problems, it often exacerbates others. For sustainable, positive, self-perpetuating change to occur, it needs to be managed well, and it needs to meet the needs of the present without compromising the future. Change puts new demands on our creative problem-solving abilities, on the way we relate to others, on

1

systems we have come to rely upon, on our abilities as a human race to adapt to everything that both nature and nurture bestow upon us.

As social and environmental problems keep pace with other rapid changes, the number of leading pattern-changing social entrepreneurs has been increasing as well, and as the geographic reach of their ideas has been expanding ever more rapidly, the rate of discovering new solutions to social problems has multiplied. These are the times in which social entrepreneurs thrive; they see lack of equity, access, and opportunity and help ensure that balance and equality are core principles upon which their innovative solutions are based.

As a result, all manner of people, small businesses, corporations, and investors become involved in and attracted to the new ideas, the novel perspectives, and the potential to advance system-changing innovations. They collectively decide to take the risk of striking out in a new direction while they engage, involve, and interact with each other in a new way, involving new actions that can indeed change the world. These are the people and organizations that Ashoka calls changemakers—those who tackle social problems directly, or do so indirectly by working closely with social entrepreneurs to make their ideas a reality and their programs successful. As the number of changemakers increases, momentum intensifies, social movements are created, and social systems are transformed. "In a historical perspective, major shifts of this magnitude have occurred with regularity, fueled by grievance and galvanized by one or a few visionaries, and benefitting from the intersection of crisis and opportunity."[1]

This whole process is enormously contagious, and more and more local changemakers who have "caught the bug" are emerging. Some of these learn from and later go on to expand the pool of leading social entrepreneurs themselves. To the degree they succeed locally, they give wings to the entrepreneur whose idea they have taken up, they encourage neighbors to become changemakers, and they cumulatively build the institutions and attitudes that make local changemaking progressively easier and more respected. All of which eases the tasks facing the next generation of primary pattern-change social problem solvers. This virtuous cycle, catalyzed by leading social entrepreneurs and local changemakers, is the chief engine now moving the world toward what Ashoka terms an "everyone a changemaker" future—a world that will be fundamentally safer, more empathetic and equal; happier and more successful than the one we live in today. A world where the word *tomorrow* begins to infer a better day to come.

Backstory

Some people watch it happen.
    Some people say, what happened?
    Some people say, did something happen?
    Some people didn't even notice that something happened.
    Some people just make it happen.
—ANONYMOUS

A number of years ago, I found out about Ashoka through a colleague of mine who applied for a job there. She called me to ask if I knew about the organization, and when I admitted I did not, she proceeded to tell me about it excitedly. Her desire to be offered the job even though it represented a foray out of the corporate sector, complete with a rather large pay cut, aroused my curiosity and triggered a recollection of something that I had heard a few years before:

If you want to do good, you have three choices:

- Become an activist or an advocate.
- Become a service provider—doctor, civil rights lawyer, teacher.
- Become a professor, researcher, or academic.

But now there seemed to be a fourth category: become a social entrepreneur.

I was intrigued by what seemed to be an interesting combination of words (social entrepreneur), and decided to find out more. I researched Ashoka and saw that though it presented itself as the largest association of social entrepreneurs in the world, it seemed to me that it was really a think tank for alternative solutions to intractable social problems. And by virtue of the collective impact of its work, Ashoka appeared to be functioning in a much larger arena—more as a hybrid organization that bridged the gap between a think tank for innovation and an action accelerator for an alternative future. I was now more than intrigued; I was hooked. I needed to know more about this new breed of social solutions innovator.

Postscript: A few months later I applied for a position at Ashoka. The rest is history—I left a rather lucrative job in the profit sector and joined Ashoka as its vice president for global marketing.

What was it about Ashoka's social entrepreneurs that so motivated me? The first thing that struck me was that they seemed to accomplish things that I always imagined I would have liked to do throughout my life. They all seemed to start out as critics. They felt strongly or indignantly about something and they gave voice to their values by translating them into action instead of ignoring the problem or complaining about it. They took the next step and did something about it. They said *yes* to themselves.

I remembered that when I was a young girl, washing the dishes while listening to the radio, I heard how the United States launched its invasion of Cuba at the Bay of Pigs (for which the attack became known in America), and how then–Soviet Union Premier Nikita Khrushchev, who was prone to slamming his shoe on the table when angered, was doing just that. This was the height of the Cold War and tensions were running high between the two countries. As a small child listening to this, I was scared.

As I continued to wash the dishes, I began daydreaming about sending Premier Khrushchev a letter that would calm him down and create peace between our two countries. I had a secret dream of saving the world and was just about to be recognized as the American girl whose letter stopped a nuclear war when my mother came into the kitchen and interrupted my reverie. I thought about that letter a few times afterward, but never sent it, much less wrote it. I ended up doing what so many people with a good idea do—nothing. So when I started to delve into the work of social entrepreneurs, I became transfixed when I realized that they all seemed to recognize that the key to making change happen was not only to imagine and articulate a sense of possibility but to visualize its path and turn it into action.

From Breakdowns to Breakthroughs

Social entrepreneurs begin by having a clear picture of the end in mind—the end being the creation of an emerging social phenomenon that cannot be reversed. They do what I always hoped I could do—confront difficult issues and actively pursue a more just, secure, and sustainable world. As they refuse to accept things the way they are, they manage to break out of current paradigms to defy convention, think counterintuitively, and rethink solutions.

They excel at reframing old thinking. For example, they use their evolved consciousness and their unambiguous sense of empathy to see autism as a "positive distraction" instead of a handicap or view people with blindness as differently abled rather than disabled—as you will see in the stories of Thorkil Sonne and Andreas Heinecke. They decipher economic structures and grasp the possibilities of microfinance—like Greg Van Kirk or

Pradip Sarmah—and turn them into new means of access to housing, commercial opportunities, and financial security. Like Mary Gordon or Abdelfattah Abusrour, they see well-trodden paths leading to violence and aggression and create space for a different reality to take their place.

They all have a great new idea and they quietly go about implementing it. Their why and their how meld together, generating a mysterious magnetic field that attracts others to them. They build virtuous cycles of sustainable mutuality by creating co-dependencies of purpose. They inspire people, they instigate others to make change, and then help them to do so as well. Humble, they are known more for what they achieve than who they are. But my big reveal was when it occurred to me that they do not sit and contemplate their actions in a "should I or shouldn't I?" way. Nor do they see their ideas as a risk. They just see something that needs to be changed and they go about doing it. It's as simple, as eloquent, as mind-blowing as that. They never seem to need to climb up to the high board; they just jump into the pool—heart first.

People often ask me whether a particular change is possible. I respond by saying that this is the wrong question. Instead, each of us needs to ask where our commitment is and where we shall act. Once we are committed, we will always find a way to be effective.

—ROBERT THEOBALD, *THE RAPIDS OF CHANGE*

Despite the subtle differences in the various published definitions of *social entrepreneur*, there is more agreement and overlap

6

than discrepancy around the notion that these people cause disruption while repositioning systems to better support equity and create significant social change. However, some nuances focus more on the *what* that is accomplished and its uniqueness and others combine the *what* with the *who* is accomplishing it.

In the end, most of the definitional disparities are evolving toward each other, and the slicing and dicing of what type of organization effects the change—be it a citizen-sector organization, a for-profit, or a social enterprise model—is diminishing. For me, the characteristics that determine the person and the motive behind the innovation become the foundation that needs to exist before any of the definitional nuances can be overlaid.

Many people tend to call anyone who starts an organization that does something for others a social entrepreneur. Though I do not necessarily consider that type of person a social entrepreneur in the "innovative, solutions-oriented, world-problem-solver" mode, I do consider all of them to be social changemakers or social-solutions innovators—that is, people who create, develop, or build an organization or a business based on a value proposition that delivers actions on behalf of others in exchange for huge self-satisfaction, with limited personal financial gain. Another genre of social changemakers and changemaking entities are those who work with social entrepreneurs and help them spread their innovations and impact to other places, people, and sectors. Be they individuals, corporations, or donors, they keep the work alive, vibrant, and meaningful. These are the people and the entities who step in to share the burden of shouldering the work involved in changing the lives of others.

Ashoka delineates the social-entrepreneurial endeavor more completely as a process that must also be enormously contagious (in the non-health aspect of the word) and self-replicating, and therefore more likely to be successful. To make the completion of the virtuous cycle happen, it will be imperative to increase the proportion of humans who know that they can cause change. This will inevitably lead to a multiplier effect that will, in turn, nourish an ever-increasing supply of changemakers. It is those current and future changemakers and the social entrepreneurs they work with that this book explores.

When Dreams Defy Reality

Currently, social entrepreneurship is as much a field as it is a social movement. A whole new generation of ethical change agents—whether in business or academia or the media—is building a new sensibility about the way we live and interact. For many people, "social entrepreneurship is now a viable and desirable career path, where work is not just something that you do, but rather something that you are."[2]

All of Ashoka's Fellows (the people Ashoka deems to be leading social entrepreneurs and elect into a lifelong Fellowship of like-minded people) ripple their innovations through society by influencing other social entrepreneurs, the policy development process, and the actions of the private sector. As I came to know the Fellows I interviewed for this book, I found that they all, at a minimum, possessed four inherent qualities:

- Purpose
- Passion
- Pattern
- Participation

These characteristics have become my favorite manner of determining if the person is starting out with the defining characteristics of what constitutes a social entrepreneur.

Purpose

I have never met an Ashoka Fellow who did not put society above personal interests and was not firmly focused on the fulfillment of their chosen role. Fellows may take many roads to get there, but the goal is sacrosanct—and they do not get sidetracked by the boulders strewn on the path. Their clarity of purpose is often the decisive factor that brings individual and organizational efforts together. This is because it defines why they are working toward something and why it is worth working on it collectively. Purpose becomes the invisible glue that connects different actions and actors while it bonds everyone with inspiration. It infuses boldness and calculated risk and it creates loyalties by helping people understand why their contribution is valuable and valued. Purpose mitigates fear and allows inspiration to replace fear with action. Purpose leads to a sense of possibility.

Passion

I am not sure if I can separate the passion from the purpose because I have come to believe that both are always present, tightly intertwined and inextricably linked together. Like strands of DNA (which passion and purpose may actually be part of) you cannot pull them apart. Passion connects to spirit and relates to strength—strength of character, of determination, of connection to others. It kindles and nourishes a "follow one's heart" courage of judgment. Ashoka Fellows have taught me that real strength lies not in the physical realm but in an indomitable spirit, intense passion, and determination aimed toward goals.

Pattern

The entrepreneurs in this book all decorate their own innovation in patterns. They base this on purpose, passion, and personality. But in a bigger sense, these patterns become models or guides for others to follow. The particulars of their patterns differ greatly, and in fact that individuality is the nature of an entrepreneur. They cultivate new ground and put together new combinations of solutions—or maybe they come up with just one that no one has ever configured in such a way. I'd like to say that they "build a better mousetrap"—but in essence, they eradicate the need for mousetraps altogether by figuring out a way to decrease the populations of mice!

Instead of just trying to alleviate the symptoms of problems, their organizations are trying to find the societal patterns that will unlock the clues to solving the underlying issues. To create significant and long-lasting changes, social entrepreneurs must understand and often alter the social system that creates and sustains the problems in the first place. This way of looking upstream toward solving the root cause of a problem is far more sustainable than looking downstream by trying to put a patch on the outcome. To borrow from public health parlance, "It is not enough to cure the symptom—for a cure to be sustainable, you must treat the underlying illness. If not, the cycle between cause, symptom and illness will continue to evolve causing a spiral of exacerbated and related problems."[3]

Participation

The Fellows discussed in this book all exhibit leadership abilities. They are often unanticipated leaders, but whether they perceive themselves to be leaders or not, their ability to influence people and have them believe, follow, and join is an attribute that is completely natural and a necessary component for impact. It is that quality that attracts involvement and eventually morphs into civic engagement.

Certainly our 2011 current events lesson on the strength and accomplishment of civic participation in Egypt should make it obvious why this last characteristic plays such a huge part in an Ashoka Fellows program. As an old but true adage goes, "There is no strength like strength in numbers." The role of the citizen, of the parent, of the child, of the street vendor, of the teacher, of the government official, of the person who is differently abled or who has positive distractions in changing an entrenched cultural pattern are all of significant consequence. It is as much the number of participants as the quality of the participation that is essential for supported and sustained social change to take place. To think boldly, act locally, and scale globally, innovators need more than their efforts as individuals; they need to get multitudes of people involved in seeing their vision, believing in the possibility, actively supporting it, and participating in creating change themselves. Leading social entrepreneurs know that if they are going to make a scratch on history, they can't do it alone. There is a point when they all know they must step back and let go of any ego-limiting ownership of the idea if they are to involve and instigate the rise of changemakers who can help spread the seeds of change and grow them into a movement.

The ability of social entrepreneurs to scale their programs depends on the strength of people's participation and their capacity to create movements that are strong enough to shake the foundations of poverty and inequality the world over. But what really makes social entrepreneurs unique? Where do they get their inspiration and passion? How do they convert that inspiration into purpose and who empowers them to think in such new ways? How do we clone these people so that we end up with a better world for all?

The Rise of Unanticipated Leaders

The magic starts when the life cycle of an idea and an entrepreneur intersect. Some would call it the aha! moment or the turning point. All of the social entrepreneurs introduced here started out on a totally different path in life—and upon turning a corner came face to face with their life's passion and purpose. They did not foresee this, predict it, or expect it, nor for the most part did they understand it—at first. Isaac Durojaiye (DMT Mobile Toilets, Chapter Three) was a Nigerian security guard, and Ursula Sladek (EWS, Chapter One) was "just a German housewife" on the mend from a broken thighbone when their purpose struck. But somehow, the switch relating to external compassion paired with the sensory receptor for internal passion flipped on, and it just seemed that setting out to refute conventional wisdom and logic to tackle an entrenched social problem was a natural path to take. So too becomes the path of many who either work with social entrepreneurs or have had their lives changed by them.

The past few years have seen a surge of good books and articles on the work of social entrepreneurs around the world—including the most popular among them, David Bornstein's *How to Change the World* and his current *Social Entrepreneurship: What*

Many of the social entrepreneurs that I have the privilege of knowing are themselves more often than not unanticipated leaders, meaning that they had never envisioned their future to be their present.

—BILL DRAYTON

Everyone Needs to Know, co-authored with Susan S. Davis. And in between, John Elkington and Pamela Hartigan wrote *The Power of Unreasonable People*, which focuses on "the phenomenon" of social entrepreneurship mixed with market-based solutions to social problems.[4] Each book talks about different facets of social change—from defining what a social entrepreneur is and how to think about becoming one to how the movement is generating new transactional models that are changing the face of business around the world.

Rippling takes you in yet another direction and explores the five strategic ways that social entrepreneurs change social systems—inclusive of both social business and citizen sector models. Its focus is on the virtuous cycles of change that make each of these ways stable and sustainable. It examines the cutting-edge thinking that accompanies an ability to turn the status quo and conventional wisdom on their heads and re-imagine a new paradigm for the way things should be. Part One: Restructuring Institutional Norms, shows how old patterns interact, interrelate, and evolve into new standards of socially beneficial practice; Part Two: Changing Market Dynamics explores the synergistic opportunities created when business success and social values creatively combine; Part Three: Using Marketing Forces to Create Social Value, and Part Four: Advancing Full Citizenship reviews the large-scale changes that arise as a result of expanding choices, options, and empowerment for people to whom these have not been traditionally and culturally bestowed. Lastly Part Five: Cultivating Empathy considers in a myriad of unusual settings, how creatively exposing youth to encounters with individuals unlike themselves and helping them replace anger and aggression with more balanced emotions are severely diminishing and even reversing their tendency to judge people as "others." *Rippling* emphasizes how these approaches literally turn "what is" and "what if" into "what can be."

There Are Many Seeds in an Apple ... But How Many Apples Are in Those Seeds?

Poverty is messy, and social problems are often the underlying cause of social unrest. They foment dissension, discontentment, and agitation. As the chasms between countries, societies, and socioeconomic classes expand and become more widespread, it is now more imperative than ever for us to challenge a larger percentage of the population to address them straight on. In support, Ashoka has argued that while the early stages of the social entrepreneurship field focused on finding and supporting leaders of social innovation, the new goal of the movement is to create an "everyone a changemaker" society where people everywhere feel empowered to create change.

The five sections of this book represent five ripples in the pond of poverty, inequity, and inadequate access to opportunity. For each system-changing example, the inspiration, the innovation, the local and global impact, and the voice of the changemakers are clearly articulated. This particular confluence of elements creates virtuous cycles of social benefit that begin when people become agents of change themselves and then influence others to do the same. They set off self-perpetuating waves of motion that convey transformation both vertically and horizontally, now and into the future. In Isaac Durojaiye's case, one of his franchisees—a single-woman head-of-household leasing fourteen toilet franchises—was able to put all her four children in school as a result of the money she has made as a franchisee, and two of them are going to the university. A fabulous accomplishment in itself—but the rippling truly starts when her oldest son, who is about to graduate from the university, comes to Isaac to ask his help in applying the franchised-toilet model to a public street-cleaning program he wants to develop with the shopkeepers in the Lagos marketplace. Public street-cleaning in Lagos? How many children brought up in adverse conditions would have thought of such a huge, culture-shifting idea? Probably none who had not been influenced by or involved in a social entrepreneur's world. The changemakers and the people they have the capacity to affect in their own daily circles will now expand Isaac's idea and use it to spread ripples in Africa's social and cultural pond.

Beyond the social entrepreneurs profiled in this book, the unseen and next-generation changemakers are in many ways the champions of this movement. The corporations who embrace a new and more sustainable way of doing business. The donors who want their money to effectively and ethically impact people's lives. The everyday people, who—no matter what culture they live in, no matter what socioeconomic group they find themselves a part of, no matter how little they possess—are trying to make a better life for themselves, their families, their neighbors, and their communities. They may live in and with poverty, but they do not possess a poverty of imagination. They have hope, and they believe that a better world is possible. Most important, they eventually end up taking action, either by themselves or with the help of social entrepreneurs. Along with entrepreneurial leadership, these are the people who form the new infrastructure that leads to the establishment of the innovation and transforms it into a social institution. The pride, empowerment, and value that changemakers feel about themselves ripple outwards and create a cycle of influence that becomes far greater than anything they could accomplish alone.

The best way to predict the future is to create it.

—DIVINE BRADLEY

And just how does social system change happen? How does the quest for fair wages for Nicaraguan coffee farmers grow into the "Fair Trade" movement in the United States? (Paul Rice, Chapter Five.) How does a Buenos Aires psychologist's concern about recidivism rates in a mental hospital result in a Saturday afternoon radio program run by mental patients that has over 3 million listeners in the Buenos Aires area alone and now is becoming acknowledged and copied all over Latin America as a way of reconnecting and integrating the mentally ill with society in a significant and sustainable way? (Alfredo Olivera, Chapter Fifteen.) How does a Canadian social worker who is deeply disturbed by the increase in bullying in schools develop a world movement around the pedagogic inclusion of empathy as an effective reducer of childhood aggression, predicated on bringing tiny babies into the classroom? (Mary Gordon, Chapter Sixteen.)

Throughout all these programs and others discussed in the book, the five distinct approaches to system change fuse with the substantial contribution of changemakers to create a force field that helps transform a solution for a geographically relevant need into part of a panacea that works for the world.

The events of 9/11 changed the world—it is now up to us *all* to change it for the better. If this book speeds you along your journey to become a changemaker or encourages you to be more of one, please let me know and share your change at www.changemakers.com/Rippling.

The World is my Country, all mankind are my brethren and to do good is my religion.

—THOMAS PAINE

Restructuring Institutional Norms

The *institution* in these chapters refers to an institution of practice. The *practice* mostly involves those that limit personal or economic freedoms and encourage and support traditional thinking that stifles new and creative ways of relating to the ever-evolving world we live in. As the world progresses ever more rapidly, why are human rights, economic rights, and ecologic imperatives lagging so far behind? Why are so many institution and industry norms still responsible for marginalizing huge portions of the world's inhabitants, and how can we provide or create access to opportunities that would add value to the lives of those who are discriminated against and disenfranchised?

In re-creating an established societal or cultural norm as well as an industry practice in some way, shape, or form, each of the Fellows in this section asked those big audacious questions. They were able to channel their indignation, disappointment, sadness, or anger into a response that satisfied their sense of equality and fairness and fueled their transformation into global citizenship.

Here are four examples of industrial, institutional, and age-old practices that got rethought, reinvented, revamped, and ultimately validated as a new way of doing business.

REFLECTIONS BY ESTHER DYSON

Why is it so difficult to change social and institutional norms? It's because no one recognized a problem as an opportunity—as in the story of the Rickshaw Bank in Chapter Three. It should be relatively simple to make change in such cases, but not always. More often, someone benefits from keeping the situation the way it is, and the best approach is negotiation—figuring out how to share some of the benefits of the change. For example, in Chapter Four, Women's Human Rights, when a woman's husband dies, she becomes available for other people to take advantage of—whether as her mother-in-law's servant or her brother-in-law's de facto sex slave. But these are circumstantial situations: Any woman could become a widow; any man could die and leave his wife as a widow in the same dire situation. Getting people to see the situation from a different point of view is key—whether from the point of view of society as a whole, or from the point of view of "this could be me."

And then there's the situation where some people actually do benefit, persistently. There again it's a question of negotiation, pitting the interests of a larger number of people, or of society as a whole, against those of specific groups or individuals. How can you share the benefits of the change? The allocation depends in part on who has power, and in part on fairness. Of course, outsiders may differ on what is fair. We are operating in the real world here.

So, in the end, the challenge is deeper: We need to change how people think: not just what they notice, which is hard enough, but also their perceptions of justice and propriety. In many cases, such as ineffective education, few people benefit from the current situation, but they just can't imagine things any other way. They think that the current order of things is the right order of things. I call that the haircut problem—a well-known phenomenon in certain segments of certain societies. Tell someone that you like their new haircut, and they immediately think: "I must have looked horrible before or they wouldn't have said anything."

Anytime you prefer a new haircut to the old one or anytime you ask a society to change, you are implicitly criticizing the way things used to be. People don't like being told they are not perfect—especially by outsiders. If you call their basic assumptions into question, you are telling them that they have been wrong or unjust, prejudiced or ignorant. The trick is to honor the past (or the present) while talking about the benefits of the new arrangement. That can be hard to do. It takes not just cleverness but also courage—even as you lead. The people in this section have that courage.

Esther Dyson is a former journalist and Wall Street technology analyst who has created several well-known publications on technology, along with the successful PC Forum conference. Dyson and her company, EDventure, specialized in analyzing the impact of emerging technologies and markets on economies and societies.

CHAPTER 1

Power to the People — Germany

Ursula Sladek is a founder of Elektrizitätswerke Schönau (EWS), one of the largest eco-electricity providers in Europe, and the largest that is run by citizens. EWS's aim to decentralize and democratize the energy supply makes it the nucleus of a continuously expanding national network of independent power generators utilizing a range of technologies.

ONE OF THE CHURCHES IN SCHÖNAU, A SMALL TOWN OF 2,500 inhabitants deep in the Black Forest region of Germany, has a very high tower. If you climb up and look out over the town at the right time of day, all you see are hundreds of solar panels reflecting the light and winking back at you. You can almost feel them blinking, "We did it, we did it. We broke the power monopoly. We are our own power source, we are the source of light in the Black Forest."

Not coincidentally, Schönau is where Ursula Sladek and her family live. But Ursula's family does not consist of only the usual suspects. Besides her husband and children she has thousands of other "family members"—all owners, comrades, and members of Elektrizitätswerke Schönau (EWS), the electric power company she created more than twenty years ago to replace nuclear and coal energy with renewable sources. From Ursula's perspective:

> Energy issues are very, very interesting because it's an issue for the whole world. Not only for Germany or Europe, it's really for the whole world. In the end, it will also be tied to whether we will have war or peace. If you think about climate changes, there will be millions of people migrating to the rich, highly industrialized countries due to drought, floods, heat, or cold making it difficult to live in their own countries. It is the developed nations that have the highest CO_2 emissions, but it is the poor countries that feel the impact on the climate the most because they have to live in it. These will be the victims of the climate changes more than we.[1]

Just a Housewife

Chernobyl was Ursula's turning point, Fukushima her tipping point. Separated by twenty-five years, both nuclear disasters have served to bring the energy issues of this planet to the forefront of people's minds. In 1986 Ursula was a self-described housewife. Like many Europeans, she was concerned and fearful about the close proximity of Chernobyl and the disaster's effects on her town, her environment, and her children.

Ursula was sidelined with a broken thighbone at the time of the Chernobyl nuclear leak. As radioactive particles landed on sidewalks and streets not far from her home, she watched her children playing outside with an anxious heart. It was at that moment that she knew she needed to get the worry of nuclear fallout out of her life and vowed to see the end to energy sources rife with unintended negative consequences. With her husband and community friends she founded Parents for a Nuclear-Free Future to ensure a safe alternative for their children.

As she told a German newspaper, "We were naïve enough to believe that energy policies and the energy industry would change after Chernobyl.... But nothing changed at all. So there was no alternative but to roll up our sleeves and take matters into our own hands."[2]

For the next thirteen years Ursula and her widely extended family would work to influence both residents and politicians on why and how to reduce energy consumption and opt out of nuclear power. They learned all about generating as well as saving energy. Within that space of time, they finally won a referendum that allowed the town to separate from the national power grid and develop its own sources of renewable energy.

After the long journey to victory was over, Ursula realized that the measure passed in large part because the citizens of Schönau were confident that they could achieve something others had always said was impossible. And if the town could do it, maybe she could do something similar.

As she explains:

I was just a housewife and a parent. I was quite shy and had never really done anything like this before. I had no business experience, I was not a scientist. I started by taking one step at a time.

24

So in 1991 she spearheaded the effort to buy the local power grid (the electrical transmission and distribution network) and set up a new company that would replace it. It was Germany's first cooperatively owned power-supply company and one of the first in Europe. Six years later, Ursula and her band of "electricity rebels" (so named by the media) managed, within a rather short time, to magically raise the money from all parts of Germany to buy their grid.

In 1998 I was already fifty years old. I had to learn how to use a computer, how to speak in public, how to run a company; all of which was something quite new for me. But I found that if I asked my friends who owned companies for advice on how they managed this and that, I could learn from the best of them. I tried what they told me and it either worked or it did not work. If it didn't, I asked somebody else. I needed to learn everything I had to do.

Building block heating stations and installing solar panels as a start, EWS began to produce some of its own energy. The hundred-year-old monopoly of large power companies in Germany was broken and EWS was poised to influence the entire structure of the electricity and power industry. Just one year later, Germany deregulated the energy industry (coincidence?) making it possible for EWS to sell its renewable energy across Germany. Within the wink of a solar panel, EWS went national.

Replaceable, Rethinkable, Reinventable, Renewable

When your mission is firmly grounded in social change, you have the freedom to reinvent your business in ways that allow for participation of those who can help you mobilize a movement. True to EWS's primary goal of decentralizing and democratizing the energy supply, Ursula decided to make the company truly

25

public—people who would invest in the company would become owners and have a voting share in company matters. Great idea, but first she had to motivate townspeople to invest their money by educating them about all facets of renewable, nuclear, and coal power, persuade them to take part in creating and finding renewable energy sources, and convince them that this would be a good investment for their money.

This hybrid social model is not at all common in Germany— nor for that matter in most parts of the world. But early on, Ursula realized that to start a movement you need people, and lots of them. They have to be invested intellectually, emotionally, and financially. Her model allows for everyone in the town to take part in the solution to their energy needs, and to take charge of their future. All get to be components of the change, elements of the revolution. All get to be changemakers in as small or large a way as they want and can manage.

EWS started in 1997, in one town with 650 local members. It is now owned cooperatively by 1,500 members and supplies power to 120,000 households, representing 250,000 people across Germany. The source of all their energy is green, mostly from hydropower operations, but also solar panels, wind turbines, and small co-generation plants in people's homes. Members can use the energy they produce for their own purposes and sell the extra electricity to the grid. The company's member shareholders receive dividends, but all the rest goes into new renewable power plants and training and supporting communities who want to run their own green energy projects, modeled by Schönau.

Cooperatives inspired by EWS are springing up in small cities all across Germany. Even larger cities like Stuttgart are deciding to take their grid and energy supply in their own hands. Many towns are partnering with EWS to develop their cooperative model and get citizens involved as members from the beginning. Global inquiries are coming from everywhere—Italy, the Netherlands, Japan, Korea, Chile, the United States, and Canada all have sent representatives to Schönau to see if the model could be used in their own countries. Ursula gets requests for more than a hundred speeches a year. A few years ago, Ursula was in Japan and gave sixteen speeches within three weeks. Sadly, she was not able to convince the Japanese to loosen their dependence on nuclear power, but since Fukushima she has been receiving so much renewed interest in that country that she made available her "100 Good Reasons Against Nuclear Power" booklet in Japanese. She has just been invited to speak at the Global Conference for a Nuclear Free World taking place in 2012 in Yokohama, Japan.

One Solution Fits All

Ironically, the recent financial crisis worked to Ursula's advantage. She has started to notice that instead of individual citizens coming to her asking how to replicate EWS in their town or city, she is now getting inquiries from town administrators and politicians who have been observing what Schönau has done and want to buy back their own grids. But interestingly enough, they now have two equally persuasive reasons for doing so. Like EWS, they want to have a higher percentage of renewable energy and self-determination. But secondly, they realize that if the large power companies control the system, the money and profits go to them, but if you operate your own grid you keep that money in your town's pockets. Since all communities could always use additional financial resources, these two complementary capabilities tip the value proposition in favor of an eco-friendly, community-owned power supply chain where environment, control, and financial reward become powerful but integrated motivators. However, though the municipalities are ready for change, they need mentorship and an experienced partner to be an effective changemaking entity, so they turn to Ursula and EWS for help. Once they ask if EWS wants to partner with them, Ursula's prime condition is that they institute a cooperative model so the community inhabitants are fully involved in the new grid as co-owners and co-changemakers.

What's interesting is that instead of working with citizens to force the change from the bottom up, Ursula is now working with the government and administrative bureaucracies, coming at it from the other direction. The model is getting to be so successful, financially rewarding, and environmentally sustainable that it is attractive to citizens and governments alike.

Mobilizing the Normal People

From her perspective, Ursula is thrilled with EWS's trajectory. In 2009, her publicly owned company was worth 67 million euros; in 2010, around 82 million. She is hoping to serve 1 million customers in the next few years. Twenty-five years after Ursula stopped being "just a housewife," she is still convinced that it's the citizens, the so-called normal people, who are at the core of the model. She knows that they need to invest not only financially but also behaviorally in creating and using renewable sources of energy themselves. For example, EWS encourages people to install a windmill or some solar panels to generate power, and EWS gives them the support they need to do so. Ursula feels that when people invest their money in cooperatives they will realize the returns both financially and environmentally:

> In the end, the change from nuclear and fossil energies to renew-
> able energy is such a great task it really needs everybody. It is so
> very important to motivate the people to take part. You cannot

just say well, the government should do it or the power suppliers should do it. Governments have a great influence on other governments and big power companies, but it is not so easy for them to do something so outside the normal way things have been run for the past hundred years. So it needs the people. And that is what is happening in Germany because there is such a large anti-nuclear movement.

At sixty-four, Ursula is still pushing the renewable energy agenda whenever and wherever she can. The five news headlines that follow give you a sense of how busy she has been. In the past few months, Germany has decided to close down all of its nuclear power plants. Coincidence? You decide.

CNN News, Nick Glass, September 26, 2011	Ursula Sladek: The Housewife Who Powered a Green Revolution
AP, Associated Press, May 30, 2011	Germany Decides to Close Down Nuclear Power Plants by 2022 "Chancellor Angela Merkel said she hopes the transformation to more solar, wind and hydroelectric power serves as a roadmap for other countries."
Guardian.co.uk, May 21, 2011	Ursula Sladek—The Power Behind the Green Revolution "British green campaigners often point to Germany as a showcase for renewables—as if this were down to an enlightened government. Sladek's story suggests that the change was actually a grass roots one, with families and communities working together."

Spegiel Online International, May 30, 2011	"On Saturday, tens of thousands of people took part in anti-nuclear demonstrations in 20 German cities, demanding a speedy phaseout of atomic energy."
Online.WSJ.com, May 30, 2011	Update: Germany to Drop Nuclear Power by 2022
	"Lawmakers from Merkel's coalition parties said that the power-generation gap would ideally by filled by renewable energy sources and relatively climate-friendly gas-fired power plants."

CHAPTER 2

The Teaching of Teaching—United States

Aleta Margolis is executive director of the Center for Inspired Teaching in Washington D.C., which she founded as a third-generation Washingtonian eager to help a struggling public school system.

I'm always ready to learn, though I don't always like to be taught.

—WINSTON CHURCHILL

ON EXITING A CENTER FOR INSPIRED TEACHING INSTITUTE, SOME OF the teacher participants said that the Institute instructors really didn't teach them anything; they had figured out for themselves how to be great teachers. Perfect! Aleta Margolis thought it was the best compliment she ever received. Now the teachers were owning it: now they knew that figuring out for themselves was exactly how to get students empowered and involved in learning. Aleta explains,

> *Now the teacher understands that it's not about the instructor or pleasing the teacher or even having a smart teacher. It's about the tenth grader saying, I'm so smart, because I figured out how to do it by myself and I spend all my time in school thinking and figuring out things and building on what I did yesterday. I have no idea what my teacher really does, but I know he is important because he helps me get there. It's not about my teacher; it's about me, the learner.*

For Aleta, that's what Inspired Teaching is all about. The Center for Inspired Teaching aims to help teachers figure out how to encourage students to enter complicated situations and devise solutions, how to think about and anticipate problems, how to turn challenges into opportunities, how to celebrate creativity and different ways of thinking. Those skills aren't high on the usual school priority list. When Aleta discusses the achievement gap affecting today's students and schools, she is convinced that it is preceded by a creativity gap.

A New Generation Needs New Ways to Learn

The role of the Center for Inspired Teaching is to help teachers learn how to encourage and mentor students to think creatively, anticipate obstacles, and devise solutions for complicated problems. Its underlying philosophy about children, and all people, is that they are inherently curious and each one deserves to be valued. Everyone is born intellectually curious and eager to learn. The school's job should be to fuel that curiosity, not to dampen it; never to extinguish it. If you want to fuel kids' curiosity and you want to channel that curiosity into learning, you have to teach in a very different way from what is being done now. The Center is grounded in a child- and teacher-centered philosophy, as opposed to one that teaches simply curriculum adherence and survival skills to get teachers through the school year. And though Aleta's program does indeed find it necessary to include some survival skills (what teacher doesn't need some?), survival is considered a secondary skill set, not the primary one.

Aleta well understands the tough accountability challenges that teachers and school districts face, not only in the United States but around the world. Everyone agrees that professional development and teacher training is important, but what's really important is getting it right. It's not about giving a new teacher a bag of tricks to survive, or a random workshop here and there that is disconnected from the realities of the classroom. It's about helping teachers develop the mind-set and the practices that are going to sustain them for a long time in the classroom. It's about internalizing teaching as a profession. Aleta feels that teaching actually *is* like rocket science. It's challenging, it's stimulating, and, like rocket science, it can be learned. She understands that teachers don't just wake up one morning and figure out how to teach. They can learn

34

how to do it, and possessing that knowledge inspires them to grow as professionals.

The traditional school model dictates that the teacher knows everything, the teacher provides the information and the correct answers, and the child's job is to absorb it all. Inspired Teaching sees a different picture. They see the child coming to class with ideas and experience, questions and knowledge. They see a teacher with exceptional skills for building, refining, focusing, expanding, and directing the knowledge the child already possesses. In fact, the picture hardly displays the teacher at all, because the Center believes that a great teacher is as close to invisible as possible. Just occasionally the teacher is asking a question, and the question might be something like "Why did you do it that way?" or "What have you learned so far?" "Have you tried that one?" "Now what do you think?" The teacher is asking challenging questions so the students articulate and synthesize their learning and get coaxed to the next level, especially when they seem to be taking the easy way out. When these children run home to tell their parents that they built their own bridge, they solved the mathematical problem required to do it, and now—finally—the bridge works, they do not say that their teacher taught them how to do it, or that they did it with their teacher; actually they never mention their teacher at all.

Moving the Deck Chairs

Since somebody's getting paid to teach in every classroom in the country and somebody's being paid to train all those teachers, every teacher either gives or receives some sort of training. So it's possible to change the entire system by just changing what we ask teachers to do, how we ask them to do it, and how we equip them for the change. If you are a smart, thoughtful person you didn't go into teaching to read a script, or to become a traffic cop in the halls, or become the enforcer of a rules-and-reward system. You became a teacher because you thought science was fascinating, because you thought language was fascinating, because you thought kids' brains were fascinating. It's not about getting the right teachers—the schools are full of them. It's about having them do the right things when they're in the classroom.

Aleta knows that education reformers often like to point to a few exceptionally effective teachers and bemoan the fact that there aren't more of them. As a result, many school systems find themselves stuck in a cycle of trying to hire more great teachers and trying to fire all the bad teachers, without rethinking what they ask teachers to do and how they train them to do it. This approach certainly doesn't appear to be leading to positive change for students. And here is the crux of the issue—it's not the teachers who aren't exceptional—it's the way they are teaching that makes them unexceptional. The role of the Center for Inspired Teaching is to help everyone in the education chain, including students, become exceptional at changemaking. This would create such a profound and sustainable impact that cities and school districts wouldn't have to tear down their school systems and build new ones. They wouldn't end up creating economic suicide by getting caught in the cycle of firing and then hiring teachers as a way of improving student performance. They wouldn't be moving the deck chairs on a sinking ship, thinking that people won't notice how bad the deck slants if the chairs are constantly being rearranged. If teachers are partners in reform instead of targets of reform, that adjustment in itself will create a more sustainable system.

Teaching Matters

Some people come to us saying I love teaching and I'm good at it, and I want to be even better. On the other end of the spectrum, some people come to us at the end of their rope, saying I'm ready to quit, I can't take it anymore, I used to love kids and now find that I hate my job. But I heard from my colleague that if I take this Inspired Teaching course, it might change how I feel, it might change what I do. I want to give it a shot.

It's no wonder that teachers and school districts are attracted to the tenets of Inspired Teaching; it's a clear instructional approach and belief system that shifts the teaching model from rote memorization to creative learning, and from giving information to instigating thought. There's a very clear technique to being an excellent teacher, and once people learn it they know that they are going to do things very differently from then on. They know they are going to enjoy their job more. They are going to work harder, but they're also going to be more motivated and know how to motivate their kids better.

Even though planning more complex, engaging lessons may make the teacher's job harder, at the same time it becomes easier because discipline problems decrease. Teachers become less worried about kids being bored and not wanting to learn because kids actually want to do the lesson. Though it seemed obvious to many for quite some time, finally, the education system is coming to recognize that teachers are important as a leverage point for systemic change. Inspired Teaching takes the concept to the next level of sophistication, investing in teachers as change agents and at the same time evolving the focus of that change from teachers to teaching.

Just recently, every U.S. state but one adopted common core standards for teaching content that children are required to learn in schools. To make sure that addressing standardized content doesn't make people adhere to the adage "teaching for the test and forgetting the rest," the Baltimore school system approached the Center to see if it could focus the Inspired Teaching methodology on building teacher capacity to incorporate the core standards into an instructional practice that fosters children's long-term understanding of the content in a meaningful way.

The two-year program would train all of the two hundred middle school math teachers in the city, the ones who deal with children at the critical age when they tend to move from an inquiry experience in elementary school to having to learn by rote. It's a unique moment in a child's life and in the teacher's as well. In an early meeting with the district's chief academic officer, Aleta remembers her saying, "After you partner with the teachers to teach differently, I want the kids to be able to walk in the auditorium and roll a ball down the sloped aisle and be able to predict the speed of the ball and the force with which it will hit the stage. I don't want them to tell me just the formula, but explain to me why." Aleta remembers thinking that their two approaches to learning meshed completely and wondered if this person was really running a school district: "How many other academic officers like her are out there? How many Baltimores can we pair up with?"

Catch and Release

Simultaneous to scaling Inspired Teaching's philosophy to an urban school district in a nearby state, Aleta has opened a school of her own in downtown Washington D.C. as part of her strategy to create wide-scale change. It's basically a demonstration site to entice and interest visiting teachers, school administrators, and education officials to see what Inspired Teaching looks like. The Inspired Teaching Demonstration School is a public charter school (subject to all the accountability and financial standards as all D.C. public schools) where master Inspired Teachers train fellows-in-residence who are studying to become D.C. public school teachers. One of the requirements for fellows-in-residence is that they commit to being changemakers; in other words, they are teachers who choose to do a different kind of teaching, and who invite people to change their way of teaching as well. At the end of the year the residents graduate from the program, become teachers, and are certified by the D.C. system. The idea is to create a virtuous cycle that continuously populates the D.C. educational system with enough inspired teachers to shift the new teaching paradigm from the distinct and separate to the norm.

Ben Frazell, a teacher who graduated from the Inspired Teaching Institute a few years ago, is now the second-grade teacher at the Inspired Teaching Demonstration School. He illustrates the changemaking capabilities of the Center's influence on the profession.

> What I enjoyed most about teaching literacy to adults who were studying for their high school GED [graduate equivalent degree] was connecting with them as equals and finding humor and joy in our time together. I decided to become an elementary school teacher because I had met many adults who had negative experiences in their own educational background so I looked forward to providing an environment of joy, challenge, and emotional support for students that would help them develop a love for learning.
>
> When I went into the classroom, I attempted to bring that same joy with me. While I was able to have many great moments and rewarding experiences, too often I felt that education had

become focused on control and conformity, both for teachers and students. I had heard that many teachers left the profession within five years, and I sometimes wondered if I would fall into that statistic. When I attended the Inspired Teaching Institute, I felt completely renewed and refreshed. Here was a philosophy where the children came first, creativity and intellect of teachers were celebrated, and the children's development was viewed in terms far larger and more significant than test scores. As I have worked with Inspired Teaching in various capacities and now as a Master Teacher at the Inspired Teaching School, I finally feel like I am fulfilled, supported, and treated as a professional. And I love working with wonderfully curious and creative students.

If Aleta gets an opportunity to influence the people who train teachers along with the people who create the expectations for teachers, then she will have gone a long way toward her goal. She knows that if a school could look different and teachers could teach differently, then students could learn more effectively, productively, and happily. But she also knows that down the road, to put structures in place that make Inspired Teaching the norm, she will have to help school districts rethink the way they evaluate teachers. This would truly enable change on a massive scale to take place. If all goes according to Aleta's vision, maybe in the future teaching and learning will be more about how well students can solve real-world problems, rather than how well behaved they are and how long they can sit in their seats.

CHAPTER 3

From Servitude to Solution—India

Dr. Pradip Kumar Sarmah, Executive Director of the Centre for Rural Development (CRD), headquartered in Guwahati, India, is a former veterinary surgeon who is helping to elevate the status of thousands of rickshaw pullers by helping them achieve ownership of the rickshaws they pull and gain access to bank loans and insurance guarantees in order to raise themselves and their families out of a cycle of generational poverty.

GIVEN MY NORTH AMERICAN BACKGROUND, I HAVE ALWAYS BEEN uncomfortable using cycle rickshaws as a mode of transportation. Not so much from a safety standpoint or a "the street comes up and hits you in your face" feeling (which it does as you are riding along), but from being overwhelmed by a sense of indignation and embarrassment that another human being should be working so hard to take me from one place to another. Observing the rickshaw driver's back as I sit behind him, I note the strain in his body as he stands on the pedals pulling my body weight. It opens a floodgate of thoughts. I feel bad that I might be too heavy for the driver; I feel too privileged, too sad that another human has to spend his life pulling a rickshaw so people dressed like me can earn a far better salary than he does. At the times when I rode a rickshaw, I remember transporting a mental image of myself to somewhere else—I made believe I was not really there.

So when I met Dr. Pradip Kumar Sarmah, founder of the Rickshaw Bank, I knew instantly that I needed to learn everything about his ideas and vision for improving the lives of the rickshaw pullers; the people for whom I felt so much empathy. He was being supportive of one of the poorest classes of people in India (as well as in parts of Asia and Africa), mostly composed of migrants from small rural villages, and I was all ears.

"People can get loans for cars, so why can't rickshaw pullers get them to own rickshaws?" Pradip asked himself this question late one night after he took a rickshaw ride to get home from his practice as a veterinary surgeon. A rickshaw was always the fastest way to get through the heavily trafficked streets of Guwahati (a premier city among the eight states of northeast India), and the only way to get to and from his appointments in a timely manner. Though rickshaws get stuck in traffic themselves, they often manage to break free more quickly than cars and, of course, they can find alternative routes prohibited to larger and motorized vehicular traffic. So for Pradip, the rickshaw was often a preferred way to travel. It was also much cheaper than other modes of transportation.

Caught in the Self-Perpetuating Cycle of Poverty

The question of ownership stayed in his mind, and one day in 2002, while he was again traveling in a rickshaw and stuck in traffic, Pradip became both talkative and inquisitive and asked the puller a few questions about his life. He found out that the driver had worked on the rickshaw for the past sixteen years, and all that time he paid about one-third of his earnings (25 rupees a day during 2002) to rent the rickshaw from the owner. But the answer to Pradip's last question was the most telling:

And the third question I asked was how much have you earned out of this rickshaw driving activity? He said around 60 to 70 rupees per day. And I asked, why don't you own a rickshaw of your own? And he said, I don't have that much money to purchase that rickshaw. [At that time, the cost of that rickshaw was around 7,000 rupees.] So by that time, I got to my destination and I got down from my rickshaw. As I go about dealing with my normal work, I forgot the whole story. But at night time, while I am going to sleep, this same story reappears to my mind. And it started disturbing me. Then I got up and I started using my calculator and I found that from all the money he paid for daily rental fees he could have been the owner of that rickshaw by the end of a year. But he never owned it, he always hired it, and because of that he could never hope to change his earning potential or his life situation. He slept on the streets and didn't have any address. He literally had no identity and because of that he was not able to get the benefit of any social services. He would never have access to any financial institutions nor to any social security.

According to Pradip, there are about eight to ten million Rickshaw drivers in India. Only ninety-nine thousand are legally licensed in New Delhi, the number of licenses capped by the city. However, illegally, there are about another six hundred thousand drivers, though no one is really sure of the exact number. Most of them have licenses courtesy of the bribery system, which extracts a 1000 percent increase in the price of a legal government license. There are no clear-cut official statistics on either the number of rickshaws in India or of the pullers who rent them. However, it is known that the Indian mafia plays a large role in the owning and renting of the rickshaws, and of collecting the fees.

Few rickshaw pullers have the initial intention of making rickshaw driving their life's work. They usually leave their villages in search of a good job in a big city and a better life. But being uneducated and from a rural environment makes it difficult to get a job. They quickly run out of the survival money they brought with them. The mafia, which owns thousands of rickshaws and on average makes thousands of rupees a day in rental fees, has appointed agents in the railway station. They can easily identify the new migrants to the city. They offer migrants a way to make money until they find a more permanent job. So the newly arrived start to drive a rickshaw. And they find that they can make enough money to get by—just barely.

These rickshaw pullers work on average eight to ten hours a day, seven days a week. In the evening they usually sleep on the street—and often get harassed by the police, so sleep deprivation is common. And since pulling a rickshaw is hard work and long hours, it's a difficult and somewhat miserable life. It's easy for them to latch onto something to make their lives more bearable. Many get introduced to drugs or alcohol as a way of relieving pain. Once they have started down this path they become addicted. And once addicted, they cannot go home or leave the city, because they need their daily drugs. They become prisoners of the city, permanent settlers who can never again return to village and family. They never get a chance to get out of a vicious cycle, and they and their dreams are crushed forever.

This cycle is happening throughout India and the addicted, street-sleeping puller is adding to the negative reputation of the rickshaw driver as a socially unacceptable person. The irony is that of the eight-million-plus rickshaws, approximately four million are running every moment somewhere on the road. On average they have two passengers, which means that eight million people are traveling in a rickshaw in India at every moment. All of these rickshaws are being driven by the rickshaw pullers. But they are never recognized as an important sector of society, a sector that is providing necessary transportation services to the entire population. They are not even considered a part of the community where they work and live.

Changing Status Quo, Changing Lives

Pradip wanted to learn more about the drivers, so in his spare time, he did a survey of three hundred rickshaw pullers. As soon as he learned enough about their plight, he submitted grant proposals to a number of agencies for funding. All were denied because the target population was migrants, and there seemed to be little interest in doing anything to help them. Because Pradip was also involved in publishing a university journal, he began to think about the income for the magazine that was generated by corporate advertising. It dawned on him that the back of a rickshaw was an ideal place to put an advertisement, and that could be a way for the puller to earn extra income.

Pradip conceptualized a new rickshaw with space to accommodate a corporate advertisement on the back. In the process, he decided to go ahead and initiated dialogue with the Design Department of the Indian Institute of Technology, Guwahati, about the possibility of such a rickshaw. Along with new knowledge and understanding of the design process, there came a ray of hope that it could be possible to create a new ergonomic design that could decrease the strain of pedaling and add to the comfort of the driver—besides providing adequate space for advertising. With these ads in the back, he conceptualized the operation of a Rickshaw Bank on the rent-to-own principle and was successful in getting three large Indian corporations to sponsor the advertisement placement costs of one hundred rickshaws, bringing the idea of the Rickshaw Bank into reality.

From the beginning, the intention of the Rickshaw Bank was to improve the lifestyle of the rickshaw drivers so they could work in comfort and with dignity. To do that Pradip realized he would have to elevate rickshaw pulling to a profession, one that people could recognize as providing a needed service that benefits the entire community. And he needed to find a way to extricate the pullers from the onerous rental fees that were ensuring that they would never be able to pull themselves out of subsistence living.

Finding a way for the pullers to pay for and own their cycles was only the entry point. Pradip's vision was expansive. It included everything from the ergonomic, advertisement-ready, newly designed rickshaw to the financing mechanism that would lead to ownership. From his original survey research, he realized that his vision would also have to include legal licensing, accident insurance, and health insurance, not only for the drivers but for the family members who lived with them. An added boost to dignity would come from supplying uniforms and photo identification cards so the drivers could look like professionals and feel pride in what they did. Pradip needed to create an entire system of dignity.

Revolutionizing the Rickshaw

The Rickshaw Bank has three dimensions that mimic the three wheels of a cycle rickshaw. One is technical, one is financial, and another is social. All three work in unison to provide an innovation that equally includes and delicately balances business and social aspects.

The technical dimension considers how best to reduce the drudgery of the rickshaw driver's work. The new model is ergonomically and aerodynamically designed; it is 40 percent lighter than traditional models, which for the most part have not changed in the century since cycle rickshaws were introduced in India. The base of the new rickshaw is lower, so it better accommodates the elderly, children, and women wearing saris. Its center of gravity is very well positioned so the rickshaw is less likely to tilt and fall over when it makes a turn at a higher than safe speed. It is much easier to drive and ride.

Financially, consider that it now costs 10,000 rupees to buy a rickshaw, and there are eight million rickshaw drivers who rent daily. Eight million times ten thousand is a big enough business opportunity to be attractive to traditional banks and insurance agencies. After getting involved in a Rickshaw Bank pilot program, four banks came forward to support the Rickshaw Bank activities. Once the banks began to understand the financial and business opportunity, they came forward to support the Rickshaw Bank activity on a large scale. And very significantly, one bank has gone even further. It is not only financing operations of the Rickshaw Bank so it in turn can keep financing the rickshaw drivers, it is also allowing the participating rickshaw pullers to open up bank accounts in their own names.

In the history of India, access to the banking system is a first-time occurrence for the rickshaw drivers. Can you imagine how powerful it must feel for the drivers to not only have the money to deposit in a bank but to be allowed to have a bank account like other businesspeople in India? It was considered by some a rite of passage with an inherently powerful societal impact.

The financial portion also includes a number of touch points. It starts with the rickshaw being given to the puller when the repayment plan begins. The driver still pays the same 24–40 rupees a day as the old daily rental fee, but that amount is considered a repayment, not rent. And significantly, the new daily repayment fee includes the cost of the rickshaw, the cost of the insurance, the cost of the license, uniform, and photo ID card. It is a payment toward participating in the entire system. And the Rickshaw Bank continues to collect the ownership installment money from the drivers and pay it back to the banks.

By aggregating the rickshaw pullers into a large pool, Pradip has been successful in the negotiations to make it all possible. For example, the rickshaw has never been insured in India. If the driver got into an accident, he lost whatever assets he had; if he owned his own rickshaw he lost it and its daily use. This was devastating to someone who had next to nothing and lived day to day. So insuring a rickshaw, the driver, and its passengers was indeed a novel idea and one that took a lot of work on Pradip's part to reassure and convince the insurance companies. Now, all rickshaws are brought under a comprehensive general insurance plan that covers accidental risk for the rickshaw, the rickshaw pullers, and the third party. By pooling the pullers and providing financing guarantees via the bank loans, the Rickshaw Bank was able to arrange for reasonable insurance premiums.

As if all this was not enough to improve the standard of living of rickshaw drivers and their families, the Rickshaw Bank decided to add a life insurance plan as well. It coordinates this program with an insurance company who has agreed to participate in the system that Pradip is creating. The premium is collected separately by the Rickshaw Bank's field collectors and again aggregated and deposited by the Rickshaw Bank's insurance coordinator. Though the initial response to this offering was not encouraging, the wives of the rickshaw pullers turned out to be very interested in it, and participation rates are increasing!

The entire Rickshaw Bank concept is designed so that by paying the same amount as their daily rickshaw rental, the drivers now make an installment payment toward ownership. They pay for a maximum of 440 days, after which they become the vehicle's owner. And then they receive the whole package, including a photo ID and a uniform, in their own name. Very interestingly, the uniform and the ID card seem to play a significant role in the whole scheme. The ID card helps keep the driver from being harassed by the police; it also helps in obtaining the health insurance. Meanwhile, the uniform adds to the professional look, which builds the driver's dignity. Both help provide well-being, physically and emotionally, while elevating rickshaw driving to a profession in the eyes of the pullers and their customers.

On the social side, the rickshaw drivers now have not only accident insurance but health insurance, and low-cost medicines are available to them. The Rickshaw Bank has become a kind of loose association to which they feel proud to belong. For the first time rickshaw drivers are doing more than surviving. And this all can be seen and felt by the public, who are now more interested to ride the rickshaws.

A New Reflection for Rickshaws

The world has certainly changed since Pradip founded the Rickshaw Bank in 2004. The word *green* has become imbued with a meaning that far transcends color. All of a sudden the rickshaw is being recognized as a green vehicle whose only fuel is human energy. The world is finally noticing rickshaws—and the rickshaw drivers and their vehicles are ready for the attention.

As rickshaws gained their newly polished place in society, Pradip added one more component to his vision. One that would change the entire system, not only for rickshaw drivers but for other workers who are considered lowly and faceless and remain unseen, underserved, and unjustly maligned. He has been petitioning the Indian government to start a fund designed to accrue interest to be passed on to banks in order to guarantee loans not just to rickshaw drivers to buy their vehicles but to others also traditionally turned away by lenders. That way, other organizations that want to copy or compete with the Rickshaw Bank can enter this newly created marketplace developed by the government's guarantee. If they get guarantees against loan defaults, then banks will be less reluctant to provide financing and the entire system of bank loans in India will be more open to people who could really use them for buying or building homes, sending their children to school, or starting small businesses.

Supporting this rickshaw revolution are the commercial and state banks, the insurance companies, and soon, hopefully, the government of India. They are the changemaker organizations who were open to seeing the social advantage of their business decision to fund Rickshaw Bank and went a few steps further because of it. They took a business risk, and they all took part in supporting a system-wide change.

The drivers who joined the Rickshaw Bank should be considered changemakers as well. They became inspired to join the Bank because they were able to find the strength of character to reject their current conditions and break out of the vicious cycle that defined their lives. By being able to dream a better life for themselves and their families, no matter how downtrodden they had become, they now became something else—they became part of the change.

Madhab Kalita is one of those drivers. He started to pull an illegal rickshaw at age fifteen and rented one on a daily basis for twenty-eight years. He felt that he had no alternative way to make a subsistence living. Now he has a newly designed rickshaw and he makes enough money that he can guarantee loans for other rickshaw pullers. He works like a voluntary agent and has helped many drivers to own their rickshaws. As his wife observed Madhab's success, she saw an opportunity for herself. She asked the Rickshaw Bank if it could help her improve her earnings as well. So the Bank designed an ergonomic cart that she could pull herself from which she could serve snacks and tea. She participated in the repayment plan and pays 50 rupees a day toward future ownership of the cart. The cart has become an informal hub, a meeting point for pullers to come to, have snacks, and deposit their daily repayment fees. She now earns more than her husband! Because of their newfound earnings, Madhab and his wife have applied for and been granted a loan from a Rickshaw Bank to construct a house. For the first time in twenty-eight years they are doing more than surviving. The cycle of change continues. . .

To fulfill his expansive vision for changing millions of lives through the Rickshaw Bank model, Pradip knows that he will have to engage many people and institutions in helping him create the required system change:

> *My vision is that the whole concept does not have to be high-tech—but bigger numbers of people, corporate entities, and civil society as a whole must be fully engaged in the concept of a Rickshaw Bank and involved in solving the issues in order to make an impact. I cannot reach those numbers alone. So banks, insurance companies, institutions, colleges, and students have shown that they*

have a role in starting similar "rickshaw banks" and in giving rickshaw pullers and owners access to loans, other bank products, and affordable insurance policies. They have a role in copying and spreading what we have done. All of them need to be part of the change and part of the solution.

The rickshaw and the system that surrounds it is an example of an informal structure that had not changed in a hundred years. There are many other similar informal and formal systems that perpetuate poverty and extract misery for millions. Access to financing, to bank accounts, to health insurance and accident insurance as well as new product and service designs can take the notion of poverty out of the dark ages. The business model developed by the Rickshaw Bank points toward emerging enlightenment.

Now that I have learned about Pradip's incredible efforts to intervene in the perpetual cycle of poverty that envelops a rickshaw driver's life and family, when I next find myself in any country where rickshaws are present, I will make a conscious effort to support them. And I will make sure to congratulate the driver on his newfound life!

CHAPTER 4

Lifting the Veil for Women Who Don't Exist—Nepal

After Lily Thapa became a widow she saw how the reprehensible treatment that culture and society foisted upon widows made them virtually disappear. She determined to reverse the age-old taboos and practices and give widows back their human rights.

> My husband was a doctor and he died in the Gulf War. That
> period after he died was a very unhappy one for me. I was so up
> and down, not knowing what I'm going to do, and I wasn't
> even normal at that time.
>
> —LILY THAPA

OVERNIGHT, LILY THAPA BECAME WHAT ALMOST ALL MARRIED
women fear most in Nepal—she became a widow. Even
though Lily came from an upper-class family and was herself an
educated and accomplished woman who ran a primary school
in Kathmandu, she instantly went from high status to almost
no status, as dictated by traditional Nepalese society. It is quite
difficult for anyone outside a conservative and traditionally
patriarchal society to comprehend that in it a woman's place in
the world and society is totally wrapped up in her decision to
marry and dependent on her husband's position. And once more,
her status is further delineated when her husband dies. Only in
the past few years, as stories of the plight of women from the Arab
world have become more widely disseminated, have people of
other cultures caught a glimpse of the tragedy of being a woman
in a religiously conservative male-dominated society.

The Woman Who Doesn't Exist

Lily was far more fortunate than most. Her family was more
modern, her parents and siblings supportive. But her in-laws, the
Nepalese law, and the society she lived in were anything but
supportive. Most women have no choice but to assume the role
decided for them by hundreds of years of culture and religion
that maintain that if a husband dies before his wife, his wife

must have bewitched him and therefore deserves to die herself. Her life without her husband is not supposed to be worth living. Under these strictures, mostly imposed by religious leaders and practiced throughout the ages, widows are not allowed to wear red, or anything colorful. They may not wear bangles, nose-rings, or any jewelry (they should not look or feel attractive). They are no longer allowed to eat meat (meat is equated to increasing sexuality). They are not allowed to live with or even near their parents (unless they were thrown out of their in-laws' home), and they are required to move in with their husband's family because all joint property previously acquired with their husband now belongs to the husband's family. In many families, especially lower-class ones, a brother-in-law has the right to exert economic, social, and even sexual rights over a widow.

It was uncomfortable for me to listen to Lily's story. No wonder she was lost and feeling "not herself"! Everything around her wanted her not to be normal, not to be herself, for in her culture only if she married again would she and her children have any rights or social or legal status. Until then, they would literally have nothing to call their own.

Lily kept on running the primary school that she started with her husband, and one day a Jesuit priest at her children's boarding school asked if she would visit another newly widowed woman who was not as fortunate as Lily and was suffering badly with her in-laws. So forty-five days after she herself was widowed, Lily went to the home of the mother-in-law of another widow whom she did not know.

When I heard Laxmi's story, it was terrible, because she was very young and had a young child. The first time we spoke she did not tell me anything. She just cried and ran. But the next meeting she told me something that always struck me. Her brother-in-law would beat up her two-year-old son if she didn't agree to share her bed with him. He left her with no choice. I was so surprised to hear these things, and I had never imagined that this could be happening to a woman here in Kathmandu. Then I came back and I couldn't stop thinking about her story. I spoke to my other friends and my family and asked how we could help her.

Lily managed to get permission from the mother-in-law to let Laxmi go to school during the day and paid for Laxmi to go to tailoring school. When Laxmi graduated, Lily bought her a sewing machine. As soon as Laxmi started to earn money and bring it home, her status with her in-laws changed. She got more respect and now her mother-in-law was the one who protected Laxmi's son while Laxmi went to work. Lily got such joy from watching Laxmi flourish that it made her feel fulfilled like never before. From then on, Lily knew what she wanted and needed to do.

Sharing Sorrows

Over the next year, widows started to gather at Lily's school on Sundays to share their sorrowful stories and get moral support from one another. Through word of mouth, the gatherings became so large that Lily had to rent a small space close by so widows could have a place to meet during the week. The meetings eventually became daily events. Lily called the space *"Bedana bisune thalo,"* the Nepalese term for "a platform for sharing." Lily and the widows added their own twist to it and called it "a platform for sharing sorrows."

Rita Thapa (no relationship to Lily), who later also became an Ashoka Fellow, was at that time an experienced program manager for the United Nations Development Program (UNDP) and a board member of the Global Fund for Women. She heard about a woman in the capital who was running a platform for widows, and—being a widow herself—she was intrigued. So she stopped by to meet Lily. After hearing about the informal meetings and all the problems the women presented, she suggested that Lily start an NGO so she could officially solicit money to expand the work. Rita helped Lily register as a legal NGO called Women for Human Rights (WHR) and then helped her get her first grant from the Global Fund for Women. Rita also supplied inspiration and encouragement to guide Lily through the process of building the infrastructure and growth capacity around *Bedana bisune thalo* so it could metamorphose into WHR.

Changemakers United

A year later, Rita was so inspired by attending the International Conference on Women in Beijing that when she returned, she quit her job at UNDP and started her own NGO called TEWA. TEWA's mission was to help Nepalese women develop sustainable local enterprises to help them earn enough to make them self-reliant, thereby elevating their status and alleviating many of the restrictions patriarchal society places on them. Its objective was to work with rural women to support their work, their political voice, and their visibility. And of course, Rita asked Lily to volunteer at TEWA so she could help mentor her on a daily basis to better prepare her to grow WHR.

> *I learned many things from Rita. How to institute programs, how to solicit grants and donations and increase funding, what all the structures of government were—everything I learned at TEWA. I started to apply what I was learning to WHR.*

At that time Lily was providing only a meeting place for widows, she wasn't actually offering any programs. After two years with Rita, Lily started restructuring her board and developing her mission and focus. Eventually Lily became the board treasurer of TEWA, and during her six years as a volunteer, she met Sadhana Shrestha, another volunteer, who (like Rita and Lily) was also a widow. Sadhana's brother worked in Sweden; upon hearing his sister's description of Lily's work with widows, he nominated Lily to go to Sweden and participate in a women's studies course. The one-month course was the final step in Lily's education. She learned how to write a five-year plan, how to raise women's voices, and how to organize groups, along with more sophisticated ways to run an NGO. She came back, left TEWA, and sold her school so she could devote full attention to making WHR what it is today.

Are You Seeing Red Yet?

In 1999, with help from Rita and many NGO groups around Nepal, WHR organized the first-ever widows' gathering in Kathmandu. It was the talk of the media as well as Nepal. Never had such a gathering of women come from all over the country as a group. And the learnings were immense. The workshop focused on two important issues: the color red and the word *widow*. Lily was well aware that the two things worked together.

> *Everybody asks me why I am focusing on the colors, because it is not only the matter of the color. But color gives you a lot of confidence. It's empowering. As soon as your husband dies, your choice of what you wear is taken away from you. So if you are free to wear anything, free to do anything, then you get your confidence back. Color is huge because it's so visible.*

But for Nepalese widows, wearing red was totally against their religious culture. So Lily reviewed all the holy books and was careful to note that nowhere were all the restrictions placed on widows written in the ancient holy books. She realized that it's all been misinterpreted, a misrepresentation regarding women and the holy books that keeps on repeating itself the world over. The widows' gathering also determined never to use the word *widow* again, as it was permeated with a sense of humiliation. They replaced it with the term *single woman*, which gave the women the ability to identify themselves as such when asked if they were married. They did not have to lie, but neither did they have to be harassed or shunned as they would be if they said they were widows.

Nepal is divided into seventy-five districts and 3,915 villages. Most are located in mountainous terrain, and if you have ever hiked the Himalayas, you have seen the precarious types of places where many of the villages are located. From its initial village-to-village, all-over-the-mountains campaign to the present, WHR has organized groups in 425 villages located in sixty-eight districts with a total paid membership of more than sixty thousand women—most under age fifty. WHR now makes catalyst grants to rural village women who are changing their communities in order to support, empower, and encourage other women to be leaders for change. They become the village changemakers, the women who change other's lives—much like Rita, Lily, and Sadhana did for each other.

Ram Devi is one of these women. She comes from a very backward, remote village. She was totally illiterate when Lily met her, and she had been thrown out of her in-laws' house with her children. WHR brought her to Kathmandu for multiple training sessions, and when she went back to the village, she opened up a tailoring shop and started to form women's groups that now number forty and have two thousand members. That was around the turn of the century, and now Ram Devi is so empowered that she is WHR's district chair. She recently petitioned and was given a land grant from the village government to build a center for women amid the orange and coffee farms that the single women have started. The profits from the farms are divided among the women and the WHR district office, which creates a sustainable cycle to perpetuate both WHR and the local women. The money is then used in a credit program to make loans to the women to build small houses.

Ram Devi has become a local celebrity. She has been asked by the local government to be on the Peace Committee, which is now one of the most powerful village committees in Nepal. Ram Devi, her village, its culture, and the lives of the widows have been changed forever. Her story represents the changes that WHR is effecting all over the country.

Widows and Half-Widows United

In 2005, Lily formed the first international conference on widows' rights in Nepal. Representatives from eleven countries attended and declared a Widows' Charter. The charter has passed to the Nepalese government and to the South Asian Association for Regional Cooperation. They adopted Article 9 and pledged that all the South Asian countries they represented would look after their widows. They are now all working on providing social security for widows.

WHR's network has now spread to all countries in South Asia with the exception of the Maldives and Bhutan, which have matriarchal societies. As Lily says with a wry smile, "Those two countries don't have a widow problem, they have a widower problem." WHR has also spread to Afghanistan to support the growing number of conflict widows and to Pakistan to support the vast numbers of widows and half-widows who are refugees. (Pakistani widows are often referred to as half-widows because they don't know if their husbands are dead or alive or where they are.) In 2010 representatives of sixteen countries attended Lily's international meeting. In 2011, in deference to the growing number of AIDS widows and those in the current fifty-four countries in conflict around the world, she appeared at the United Nations raising the issue of specifically mentioning widows in all human rights issues. Interestingly enough, there are no examples of any human rights declarations that specifically include widows.

Lily is proud of the discriminatory policy changes WHR has been able to effect. As a result of her work, the Nepalese law has now changed and widows of every age receive monthly allowances from the government every year as their social security. Lily credits Rita and TEWA with giving her the ability to free herself from the societal tentacles holding her back and the opportunity to scour the country to find changemakers. These experiences made her feel like she was a changemaker catalyst and a big part of helping Nepal rebuild after the Maoist insurgency. "Rita made me jump into that sea," she says, "and I just started swimming." And whatever happened to Sadhana, who was also being trained as a changemaker alongside Lily at TEWA? Nominated by Rita, Sadhana became Nepal's first director of Ashoka and went on to help create a culture of social entrepreneurship in Nepal that thrives to this day.

Lily, Rita, and Sadhana are extreme examples of how social entrepreneurs sow seeds of inspiration, mentorship, and role modeling; mix them with liberal amounts of innovation, support, and determination; and scatter the landscape with changemakers who for years to come will grow and sustain what they have begun.

PART 2

Changing Market Dynamics

In contrast to Part One, which explored the reinvention of the basic fabric of an industry of practice so that it transformed into something quite different, the social entrepreneurs profiled in this section use an existing marketplace concept, institution, or practice—like consignment, banking, and a commodities exchange (an actual produce market)—and shift the dynamics of that model to make it more open to those previously excluded and therefore disadvantaged by its application. The Fellows here looked beyond the existing market structure by including the stakeholders and changemakers in the redesign. Allied, they applied practical innovation and systemic foresight to open the market for themselves as well as others who can now profit from it—socially and economically. The normal and customary state of the market and the interconnections that regulated the dynamics of the system have been altered forever.

REFLECTIONS BY
PETER M. SENGE

Social entrepreneurship has become a worldwide movement in the past decade, due in no small part to the work of Ashoka. Prior to this movement, the conventional view held that there were private issues and public sector issues, and government was the steward for the latter. But increasingly the line is blurring between the sectors as it becomes clear that the challenges we face—worsening gaps between rich and poor, destruction of critical ecological support systems, failing core institutions from finance to education—are simply beyond the scope of governments to deal with alone. They need action, not talk. They need on-the-ground solutions created by people who know their local context and can get things done. But they also need solutions that can scale. They need approaches that are not so idiosyncratic that they only fit one setting or are only successful because of the gifts of particular leaders. In short, though the language might seem askew with the image of social entrepreneurs, they need theory and method—carried forward by people with a vision that their work is not just their work, that they are simply prototyping ideas and strategies for others to extend far wider than they could ever do themselves.

The stories in this section focus on learning within existing market contexts. They show how imaginative entrepreneurs have slowly but steadily fostered an evolution from a market context that excludes people to one that creates opportunities. What is involved in each is simply seeing the system that is at play on the ground and finding ways to nudge it in the direction of inclusion and enhancing social well-being. In none of the cases was there a grand plan. Instead, people got engaged, made small steps, assessed what was working and not, and adjusted their approach as they went. In short, they learned rather than figuring things out in advance—something that also invariably proves impossible when large amounts of money must be committed in advance and people become committed to programs and plans.

Lastly, the ripples from the social entrepreneur movement spread wider than the stories here would indicate—for the real changes go beyond "social" versus "business" entrepreneurs. I spend a fair amount of time in China—about one month out of the year for the past decade. There I have a teacher who is steeped in the Chinese wisdom traditions. One day he said to me, "There are no entrepreneurs in China." I said I did not understand what he meant, since there were obviously thousands of entrepreneurs by the general account. He said, no, these people only wanted to make money. In traditional Chinese culture to be an entrepreneur you must have in your heart the aim of making your society better. This is what it means to be an entrepreneur—and why he said there were none today.

This is no less true for enterprise in general, big or small. I believe there is no more pernicious common belief than that it is the purpose of a business to make money. Many years ago, Peter Drucker said, "Profit for a company is like oxygen for a person. If you do not have enough of it you are out of the game." But, I would add, if you think your life is about breathing, you are obviously missing something. Businesses who think their purpose is to make money fail to tap the spirit and potential commitment of people—and with it their imagination, patience, persistence, and creativity—large or small.

And more and more entities are starting to understand this, including some very large ones.

What big enterprises can do is different from what smaller ones can do. There will always be a need for entrepreneurs, just as there is always a need for the growth of new life at the edges of every established ecosystem. But those today we call *social entrepreneurs* may be what we simply call *entrepreneurs* in the future, just as we may come to regard enhancing well-being as one of the basics of business itself. In the end, transforming what it means to be an enterprise may be the biggest contribution that comes from the social entrepreneurs movement.

Peter M. Senge is founding chair of the Society for Organizational Learning, a global community of corporations, researchers, and consultants dedicated to the "interdependent development of people and their institutions." In 1997 the *Harvard Business Review* identified Senge's book *The Fifth Discipline* as one of the seminal management books of the previous seventy-five years.

CHAPTER 5

Using MicroConsignment to Open a Door to Economic Inclusion— Guatemala

Greg Van Kirk developed a reverse consignment model that makes it possible and feasible to offer first-time solutions to health, energy, environmental, and economic challenges to rural villagers throughout the developing world.

If microlending met charity and had a robust baby, you'd have microconsignment.

—ONNA YOUNG

MUCH OF POVERTY HAS TO DO WITH LACK OF ACCESS AND opportunity. Billions of people around the world, especially those who live in the most rural and vulnerable communities, lack any means to obtain the vital services, goods, and technologies that many of us take for granted. Without access to critical items that could dramatically improve their lives, they stay on the margin, segregated from the rest of the world and unable to escape from the cycle of poverty.

The MicroConsignment Model (MCM) creates a system of economic security and sustainability by focusing on empowering people from the community to become micro-entrepreneurs who provide services and technologies to the underserved population they belong to. It's not a completely new idea—the consignment model of business has been around for years. But Greg Van Kirk's version takes an existing model of commerce and twists it just enough to open the door for the most impoverished people to walk through and gain a chance for a better life for themselves, their families, and their community members.

The result is that both seller and buyer attain the footing they need to sustain an improved standard of living. The mission of MCM is to create first-time access to life-changing technologies—stoves, solar lights, hearing aids, eyeglasses—for rural villagers through the creation of locally owned and managed, profitable social enterprises.

You Don't Sell Ideas, You Create Ideas That Sell

How did an international banker come to live and work in Guatemala and develop this model? The story starts awhile back when Greg Van Kirk read David Bornstein's book *The Price of a Dream*, about Mohammed Yunus, the founder of microcredit (and the first social entrepreneur to win a Nobel Peace Prize due to the widespread impact of the movement he started).[1] The idea totally resonated with Greg (ah, the power of both an idea and a dissemination mechanism) and in his mind, it crystalized the application of blending business and social entrepreneurship to make an impact.

What Greg most came to appreciate was the power of counter-intuitive thinking inherent in Yunus's model. Yunus had turned a problem into a solution. That showed Greg a path, a way to do things—the elegance of designing a fairly simple financial solution that could tackle widespread poverty in a way that he hadn't conceptualized before he knew about microcredit. Being in banking, he certainly understood how to solve financial problems, and the microcredit approach seemed like a good way to tackle them for a vast amount of the world's population. So at age thirty, ignoring all the strange looks from his colleagues, family, and friends, he decided to merge his financial acumen with his social passion. He quit his banking job and joined the Peace Corps.

Greg was assigned to a small mountain town in Guatemala, seven hours from the capital, that had been hard-hit during the thirty-year armed conflict that ended in 1996. After supporting a number of existing Peace Corps–initiated village improvement projects, he decided that what the village could really use to improve itself economically was a restaurant where Peace Corps volunteers, locals, and tourists could go. Starting a restaurant was off the Peace Corps menu, so to speak, but he was persuasive enough to receive special permission to proceed—though with no extra funding.

This would have put a stop to most people's plans, but equipped with $4,000 of his own and an English-language cookbook—and with only microwave experience as a cook—Greg, along with local cooks and waiters, opened a restaurant to help bring new money into the village. From the start it turned a profit. With the glow of entrepreneurial success under his belt, he started complementary businesses: an Internet center, a trekking business, an artisan store, a Spanish-language school, and eventually a youth hostel. All of these tourist-oriented businesses were planned with and involved on-the-ground local help and management. The aim was to create local ownership as well as financial and administrative self-sustainability so that the enterprises could function on their own and support not only individual livelihoods but the town's all-around growth and well-being.

From the outset, Greg had challenged himself to devise a way to create local ownership, to find people who could understand the work and who shared the same core values. If he could be successful at accomplishing that, he was sure the enterprises he was building would prosper and thrive. Over time, he realized the secret of success was to set up localized companies and identify resident micro-entrepreneurs who would then become leaders of the business. Then, through their commitment and hard work, they would earn a share of ownership. He started by offering ownership of the restaurant to the cooks and waiters who worked there. To this day, ten years later, the businesses are all alive and well. They are prospering under local ownership and still attracting both locals and tourists.

It All Started with a Stove

One day, after donating profits from the tourism business to ten families to buy indoor cookstoves, Greg visited the villagers that had been lucky enough to get one of the new stoves. Greg was amazed at the positive impact the stove had on village families. Before getting the stove they had had to cook campfire style in their home on their dirt floor. Now they were able to work more efficiently by standing and having clean surfaces to work on. The new stove meant less wood (and thus decreased cost for fuel), less work, and no more inhaling smoke.

After observing this, Greg wanted everyone in the village to have a stove and reap the same benefits, but he realized that the donations route would never get them there. So he talked to a local mason who agreed to build a few stoves using a new and less costly stove design that Greg and the mason created. Greg consigned the construction materials to the mason so he would bear no up-front financial risk for having to purchase the materials. He then added a small margin onto the sales price so the mason could cover his labor and time and also realize a small profit. The last piece of the plan was the addition of a six-month repayment schedule for customers, so they could get a stove with hardly any money down. As they were now able to realize the savings on fuel costs that the stoves made possible, they could use that money to fund their repayments; and the stoves literally paid for themselves.

As Greg suspected, the first few stoves sold quickly. The series of small monthly payments resulted in ownership of the stove, profit for the mason, and repayment of Greg's investment money. The mason now had a brand new business venture he could grow. He could hire employees, sustain his business, and at the same time help his fellow community members get something that they had never had access to before. Equipped with a newly designed inventory-financing mechanism and with some small business training that Greg provided, the mason found that his eyes were now opened to an entirely new opportunity. He had become a new micro-entrepreneur helping people in his village, and Greg began to realize that maybe he was onto something.

Greg had discovered a new system for helping people sustain themselves by removing the burden of the risk and cost for the initial order of materials, the initial expenditure of time to create the product, or the buying of finished products. The costs to start a new business no longer had to be a barrier to market entry. People who had no money of their own to begin a business could now be presented with that opportunity. The MicroConsignment Model was born. Greg could now expand MCM from stoves to other goods and services. He and his team could now develop an entire group of micro-entrepreneurs who, as he envisioned, would make life easier and more productive for tens of thousands of people around the world. As of 2010, these micro-entrepreneurs have sold over 80,000 solutions; reading glasses, eye drops, water filters, vegetable seeds, and energy-efficient lightbulbs, solar panels, chargers, and lamps.

Profits Without Social Compromise

In 2004 Greg and partner George Glickley founded Community Enterprise Solutions (CE Solutions), a nonprofit social enterprise innovation incubator and implementation mechanism established with the goal of empowering business and educational entrepreneurs to make a difference in their communities. Its role was (and still is) to identify, train, equip, and support local entrepreneurs to provide sustainable solutions that address long-standing rural economic, health, and educational problems. CE Solutions aims to change obstacles into opportunities by converting traditional relief solutions into high-impact, locally owned and managed social enterprises and institutions.

The initial idea was to develop a complete system around empowering new micro-entrepreneurs to visit remote villages and sell products and services with a service provider approach. They would examine, explore, and familiarize themselves with needs of the community. Then, in collaboration with CE Solutions, they would figure out if there was an existing technologic solution that the villagers could use to fill the need. This would provide a service to the community, and as the micro-entrepreneurs visited more and more communities, they would identify more and more needs. Alternatively, when CE Solutions found new helpful products that were becoming available, the micro-entrepreneurs would go back to the community and see if there was a need and a market for them.

As an example of the MCM's bottom-up, solutions-oriented approach, two of its first entrepreneurs, Esperanza and Margarita, realized that quite a few people in the villages they visited were suffering from a similar eye condition. They identified a need to treat pyterigium, a noncancerous growth of the thin tissue over the white part of the eye (conjunctiva). There is no cure for this condition and the precise cause is not known, but it is aggravated by exposure to sun, dust, and smoke, all of which affect individuals living in the rural developing world. These two women identified the need for treatment and asked Greg and his team to help find a solution. As a result of this, these entrepreneurs have sold over 9,500 pairs of UV protection glasses to address this problem in remote villages.

Greg believed that MCM's simple feedback loop of information could help the women (the micro-entrepreneurs were almost always women) build a growing basket of solutions consisting of multiple products and services. You couldn't see up close anymore and now you can have an exam for reading glasses and then get the reading glasses to help you see better. You didn't have light, now you could have solar light. You were cooking on the floor and breathing in harmful smoke, now you can afford a stove with a chimney. As the market price of these products declines over time (as it certainly has with solar products) and as technology becomes more widely disseminated and more accessible, the MCM becomes more effective and more efficient. The value proposition, however, remains the same. Although people might have little money, they value these goods and services tremendously and because they perceive the need for them, they'll find the money to pay a fair price for them. In the end, the entire village prospers—not only because money is being generated among the villagers but also because productivity goes up as people now have the means to do better, stay healthier, feel better, and be far more efficient at what they are doing.

The system creates a multidirectional flow of information, which consistently helps improve the value of what is being offered and diminishes the risk for the micro-entrepreneur that the proposed goods won't be needed and bought. But the counterintuitive cornerstone of the system is that the micro-entrepreneur is not given a loan; instead, she is advanced resources as a tool for success. In other words, the micro-entrepreneurs don't have to think about the risk of having to pay for their first batch of products. They are able to buy a second batch of solutions with the money they made on the first one and incrementally, little by little, pay back the money for the first batch. To create long-term self-sustainability, CE Solutions created a local Guatemalan sister organization called Soluciones Comunitarias (SolCom). It not only buys the solutions-oriented products that are suggested by the women but pays for the first consignment of product and helps the micro-entrepreneurs disseminate it. And most important of all, at the end of all the sweat equity that the entrepreneurs put into their work, they can eventually share ownership of the enterprise.

The Power of Counterintuitive Thinking

Juanita Xoch was someone recommended to Greg as a possible micro-entrepreneur by the weaving association where she was working part time. She was shy and timid but interested in the work, so he trained her to introduce the concept of reading glasses to a group of villagers and then do eye exams for them. After her initial intimidation and insecurity passed, she ended up selling hundreds of pairs of glasses every month, doubling what she was making as a part-time worker.

Greg remembers Juanita as someone "who had gone from just being a weaver with a part-time job to now seeing herself more as a community leader." Right after hurricane Stan hit in 2005, she used her money from selling eyeglasses to start buying food for people in her community. She had so many relationships built over time from selling her products that she had a distribution channel that other aid organizations did not. She knew where the people in her community were and what they needed. She was now a respected "bridge to the last mile." She became a problem solver—not just for this one time but as future needs like this arose.

When asked how her life had changed since she began helping others through her work within the MCM, she didn't hesitate, explaining:

Before, I didn't earn enough money for family and I wasn't helping people, I just dyed yarn. Now I help people. I help my family with my earnings, I help people see better with our glasses, and I help rural people spend less money on firewood with our stoves. I like going to communities I have never visited before and learning about people living far away from the cities. I have learned about eyes; before I thought once you couldn't see, you couldn't see, but now I know that with reading glasses you can see again and continue your work. I like showing and teaching people this. Once a year I hold a meeting with the local mayors and we figure out ways we can work together and how I can go into different more remote communities. This makes me feel happy and proud.

Juanita learned to use a computer, send e-mail, and use Skype; she uses Excel, she uses Word. She has become a model regional manager, and her region became one of the most successful in the country. She has persevered, and she's helped thousands upon thousands of people in her region with access to solar lights and stoves and glasses and seeds—all kinds of daily necessities. She's become a leader, she owns shares in and is on the management team of SolCom. She's become an empowered independent woman on a mission to improve the lives of her countrymen and women.

There Are No Permanent Allies, Just Permanent Interests and Values

The key to Soluciones Comunitarias's success is aligning interests and building relationships. The MCM aligns all stakeholder interests by creating mutually beneficial relationships aimed at serving the community. The mission fosters teamwork and relationship building internally, as well as externally among the villagers. It is now owned by eight local Guatemalans who started as micro-entrepreneurs and now own 100 percent of the company. Juanita is one of the owners, along with Miguel Brito, who started off as a part-time waiter in the original restaurant enterprise and is now president of the company that owns it. All of the eight truly care about and believe in the long-term vision of SolCom and as owners they are incentivized to help it grow.

The MCM is the mechanism that creates this value chain of empowerment—empowerment through ownership, support, opportunity, and choice. The MCM demonstrates that when everyone is empowered, everyone wins, and that is the basis for everyone being able to create change. But what is fundamental is that empowerment is created by developing and offering intelligent and informed opportunities.

Greg and his team took the concepts of microcredit and microlending, deconstructed them, and flipped them over. They employed market forces to craft a win-win social business model where everybody has a role to play in the system and each one realizes benefits from the very beginning of their involvement. The model lends an outstretched hand to the most vulnerable rural communities by addressing the what (essential products and services), the who (rural villagers), the where (rural and remote areas) and by creating a how (the MicroConsignment Model); the result is a highly scalable local distribution network that works to diagnose and address the myriad obstacles confronting the most vulnerable families at the base of the pyramid. The MCM succeeds when the product, price, place, and promotion facilitate more access for people who have none, and when villagers buy what the entrepreneurs are selling and the entrepreneurs sell what their community needs and wants to buy. It is elegantly designed to fail if people aren't feeling that they are receiving value.

The Balance Between Impact and Sustainability

The MCM was designed to fill the gap for previously unknown or inaccessible products from the perspective of both the entrepreneurs and the villagers—their potential customers. MCM entrepreneurs engage in businesses where supplies never existed, perceived demand is highly unpredictable, and thus the environment is uncertain. The MCM is most effective when introducing the client beneficiaries to products and services that they need but never realized existed or never thought they could attain. Conversely, the micro-entrepreneurs would never have thought they could offer these services and products. They were mostly homemakers, often with limited education, and thought only doctors could provide reading glasses, or only men could provide stoves or solar light. Greg cannot count the times a woman has given him a "what are you smoking, gringo?!" look when he said she could start a business giving eye exams and selling reading glasses. "Who, me?" she responds. "Impossible!" "Yes, you," he replies. "With training and on-the-job learning it's totally possible!"

As Greg often says, "As long as you put the heart in the model, it will succeed." In large part, the heart is what guides the systematic approach of all of Greg's organizations. As MCM gets more widely known, organizations such as VisionSpring, which distributes reading glasses in poor communities worldwide, have adopted the MCM as a way to be more efficient with their distribution and be more empowering to their local entrepreneurs. In addition, they are also partnering with CE Solutions to see what other vision aids can be added to the basket of rural village solutions.

Since inception of the model, MCM entrepreneurs have executed more than 2,800 village campaigns and have sold more than 80,000 solutions. They have added glasses (2004), eye drops (2005), vegetable seeds (2008), energy-efficient lightbulbs (2008), water purification (2008), and solar panels with chargers and lamps (2010). Next, they will be adding drip irrigation systems. For the first time in their lives 24,500 people now have glasses, 6,100 have solar chargers and lights, 2,225 families have improved cookstoves, 750 have water purifiers, 5,100 have energy-efficient lightbulbs, and 5,900 have purchased vegetable seed packets. Greg calculates more than 120,000 direct beneficiaries with a direct economic impact of $2.75 million. And astonishingly, more than three hundred entrepreneurs have earned up to $2 *per hour* in a country where many people live on under $2 *per day!* SolCom in Guatemala is now profitable and staff have collectively earned in excess of $175,000. The model has expanded to Ecuador and Nicaragua, and in 2011 it began in South Africa, Mexico, Peru, and Egypt. To help spread and scale the model, Greg and his team have partnered with Miami University to create the Center for MicroConsignment, so others can learn how to replicate and even improve on the approach.

The MicroConsignment Model is built to fail if paternalistic or unscrupulous elements infiltrate. It involves an incredible value chain of players who help make the system work: donors, a parent NGO, product solutions providers, locally owned and managed social enterprises, micro-entrepreneurs (along with their families, peers, and communities), local mayors and community leaders, interns and volunteers, and end beneficiaries (the buyers). If there is misalignment, if any one of these actors fails or if someone is being ill served, the system will fail. It may work for a short bit, but it won't last. This nonlinear self-policing creates many gatekeepers who are responsible for letting the others in and out.

But the real brilliance of the system is that problems, needs, and solutions move up and down this human value chain simultaneously and continuously. And the MCM can be used to strengthen not only other Ashoka Fellows' projects but also the project design for anyone who has or wants a distribution system for what they are already building; they can look to this model as a way to enrich their existing plan and involve and engage many more changemakers than they ever thought possible.

While visiting Yoly Acajabon, the MCM's third entrepreneur, who is now another shareholder in SolCom, Greg became truly aware of what his work is all about:

I visited Yoly in her home, where I found her in bed and somewhat depressed. She had just had an operation and was in pain, physically and emotionally. She did not have that Yoly smile and "we will prevail" spirit I had gotten used to. I asked her how she felt, told her I was thinking of her, offered to help if I could, and tried to reassure her that she would be better soon. But none of this seemed to lift her spirits much. So I started to talk about our work together. As she began talking about the needs in her town for water filters and how we could best help meet them, she was transformed. She said, "Gregorio, I want to get out of bed as soon as possible and get out there and see if people will buy these. There is such a need!"

After leaving Yoly's house, I thought about what had happened and realized something that drives me now on a daily basis when work gets difficult. Yes, the MCM gives people access to things they need to improve their health and save money. It also creates income for women. But it is about much more than that. It gives women like Yoly a sense of purpose. It inspires hope. These are benefits we cannot quantify, and they will far outlive any of our measurable achievements.[2]

Postscript: Haiti

The 2010 earthquake in Haiti took an enormous toll on the people and the economy of the country. Because the MCM is, among other things, an elegant method for identifying people's needs and creating relevant solutions to address them, Greg recently accompanied a handful of Ashoka Fellows working in a variety of disciplines to a small Haitian town on the border with the

Dominican Republic. The town lacks health care, water, electricity, and almost everything else, and the Fellows are collaborating in an effort to identify sustainable solutions to present and future challenges. They are coordinating and interconnecting their individual entrepreneurial approaches so they can, as a team, help rebuild the town in an economically, socially, and sustainably feasible fashion. Might the MCM become a tool to get people back on their feet and help reduce poverty in Haiti? Greg is confident that it will. From Latin America to Africa and now to Haiti, the MCM may just end up becoming part of the *big* solution to end world poverty. Stay tuned.

CHAPTER 6

Dialing Maize 411—Kenya

Dr. Adrian Mukhebi is equipping poor, small-scale farmers with information that allows them to avoid exploitation by empowering them to be fully informed market participants and legitimate forces in the open market, which enables them to negotiate better prices for their goods.

DR. ADRIAN MUKHEBI GREW UP ON A TWO-HECTARE (FIVE-ACRE) FARM in western Kenya with his parents, brother, and two sisters. Nearby was the second-largest agricultural market in the country, where each year thirty thousand small-scale farmers come from miles away to trade their goods. His father was basically a subsistence farmer, but whatever produce was not consumed by the family was sold at market. Adrian remembers accompanying his father on market trips and watching him sell his vegetables and grain. He was always struck by his father's lack of control in price negotiations.

> *My father along with the other farmers was a price taker, not a price giver. The buyers seemed to have all the power to determine what prices they were going to pay. And if the buyer came and said, well, I see that you're selling tomatoes. I will pay you this much, and my father would say, but can you give me a little bit more? And the buyer would say, no thank you, and would walk off to another seller. And so—because my father needed to get some money from his trip to market to pay my school fees—he is saying, no, no, wait, it's OK, just give me anyway.*

In 2010, census results indicated that 70 percent of Kenya's 38 million people were surviving from agriculture, a field dominated by small-scale farmers. More than 70 percent of the formal and informal labor force was employed in some sort of agriculture-related work. As in many African countries, the agricultural sector has been identified as key to poverty alleviation. Despite its importance, over half the people living in rural areas of Kenya live below the poverty line, earning less than $1 a day. According to the Food and Agricultural Organization of the United Nations, more than 4 million people in Kenya (as of August 2011) do not have access to sufficient food. Although it is believed that the country has the capacity to produce enough food to feed its entire population, the government has resorted to importing food.

The Sorrows of a Small-Scale Farmer

Adrian's father made such a poor living selling his produce at market that, as is unfortunately the custom in poor families with girl children, his two sisters were forced to drop out of school and marry early so there would be enough money for Adrian and his brother to go to school. As he grew up and studied agriculture, Adrian became fascinated with how farmers market their produce and how little money they make out of it despite all their sweat and hard work. While getting his degree in the United States in agricultural economics and marketing, he took a class that involved students in buying and selling commodities—mimicking the Chicago Board of Trade. Every morning during class, he would study the *Wall Street Journal* and its agricultural price information on wheat, corn, pork bellies, and other commodities throughout the United States. The class would simulate buying and selling, and at the end of the semester the students added up how much they had actually made trading over time. Adrian ended up making quite a bit of (fictitious) money and in the process became fascinated by the world of commodities trading.

Later on, when he had an opportunity to visit the Chicago Board of Trade in person, it all clicked into place for him.

> They took me to this little museum and into a small room where there was a blackboard and chalk dating from 1848, when the Chicago Board of Trade was created by farmers who were tired of buyers offering them very low prices at market. And so the farmers got together and asked what they could do in order to get better prices. They decided they would sell collectively. They would bring their corn or wheat together, and whoever wanted to buy would pay to buy out of all this grain that the farmers had brought. They would write how many bushels of wheat or corn was there that day on the board. In this way they limited the buyers' negotiation power

and their bids resulted in higher prices to the farmers. In the end, the farmers discovered that by working together instead of competing, they had the edge over the buyer. That is how the Chicago Board of Trade started. When I saw this I knew that when I got back to Kenya, I must do this.

And so KACE—the Kenya Agricultural Commodity Exchange—was born in Adrian's mind.

A Community of Commodities

Adrian returned to Kenya with a doctoral degree, but because the Kenyan government now controlled all the agriculture prices, setting up a commodities market was anything but a simple matter. It would take him another seventeen years to fulfill the promise he made to himself at the Chicago Trade museum. His opportunity came when, influenced by the International Monetary Fund and the World Bank in the early 1990s, Kenya liberalized and privatized the agricultural sector, which ironically resulted in depressing prices and more exploitation of farmers. Now was the right time.

In 1992 Adrian registered KACE and set up a small kiosk with a chalk board in a midsize market place. He was working full time as an economist, but believed so passionately in his idea that he spent every evening and weekend building KACE from the ground up. After a short while, it quickly became apparent that not too many people were coming into the kiosk to check on prices. Adrian came to realize that the farmers were scattered all over the place and before they took a long trip to try to market at the exchange that he set up, they needed to know prices so they could tell if it was going to be worth the extra travel. They also represented so many products that it was hard to aggregate them under the few commodities that Adrian was posting. So Adrian needed to reconfigure a system that covered more markets and included more commodities.

Now, in addition to just having one trading kiosk in one town, he recruited young people and sent them to collect prices in the six major wholesale markets in Kenya, where all kinds of commodities that are produced and sold in the country are traded. He set up a system of collecting, updating, and disseminating information that has now evolved into a market information and linkage system called MILS, which offers two principal services targeting poor smallholder farmers: reliable and timely market information and efficient linkage to input and output markets.

Trees Are Not Only for Sitting Under

At one end of the MILS are market resource centers (information kiosks) located in each of the six markets where small farmers go to sell their produce. Every morning when the prices are collected and updated from each of the markets, they are sent to all of the centers via computer. The information is downloaded, printed, and tacked onto the kiosk wall.

When farmers come to the market they are encouraged not to sit under a tree just waiting for a buyer to come to them but to come to the kiosk and learn the prices in the markets so they can be empowered by that information. Now the buyers, who mainly come from urban centers, cannot cheat them. The buying and selling process is equalized: the farmers also know the prices in all the other big markets, and with this information they are able to bargain for a better price. The farmers go from passive "price takers" to active and equal "price givers." This change is exemplified in an interview with farmer Martin Kisuya. Like 2,000 farmers who daily send a simple seven-cent text message to access morning commodities prices on their cell phones, Martin can see the going rate in markets around the country.

> In Nairobi, they're selling maize at Kenya shillings 3,950 a 90-kg bag. In Kitale, they're selling at 1,600. Then in Mombasa, it's 3,300. I'll automatically get the prices of the commodities from various markets. On the whole, it has actually reduced my costs of looking for markets. Because I would not have managed to go to each and every market looking for the best prices.[1]

Another asset located at the resource center is the market linkage service. It connects offers to sell with bids to buy. Instead of sitting and waiting under a tree, the farmers are encouraged to post the amount of grain or head of animals they have to sell and have the buyers come to see everything there is to buy at one time. The pricing process becomes more transparent for the farmer and more efficient for the buyer. Through this process, fair prices are set. This was Adrian's adaptation of the Chicago Board of Trade—Kenya style: a market resource center in rural areas that provides market price information and a buyers and sellers exchange through the ease of a chalk board.

Creating a Virtual Agricultural Supermarket

Even though he was using a computer to relay market information to the resource kiosks, Adrian came to realize the geographic limitations and labor intensity of his system. Mobile phone technology was rapidly spreading in Africa, so Adrian determined to find a way to harness its power. He worked with the two largest phone companies in Kenya to upload daily price information so every morning farmers and other players in the agriculture space can now use their mobiles to download the information. All the farmer has to do is type in "maize 411" to one mobile network and "maize 247" for the other.

For farmers who are illiterate or not comfortable with mobile technology there is an interactive voice response service, which is sent in the form of a voice mail. When farmers dial the number they can hear the prices, instead of having to read them. Similarly, for those farmers, traders, and other agricultural users with Internet connectivity, information is sent to the user database electronically via e-mail messages, a website, and spreadsheet tables. But by far, the radio is still the most accessible technology for rural areas. So *Soko Hewani*, the "Supermarket on Air" radio program, was created along with a companion market call center. Information is compiled on who wants to buy and who wants to sell and these offers and bids are broadcast. If listeners are interested they call for more information and exchanges of contact information are provided. Farmer Willy Wasike Esike, from the Mt. Elgon District, attests to *Soko Hewani*'s usefulness:

> Last year I planted a lot of tomatoes. But when they were ready for harvesting I could not find buyers. Then I heard of *Soko Hewani*. So I called KACE and they placed my tomato offer on *Soko Hewani*. I immediately received calls through my mobile phone and buyers came from far to my farm. I managed to sell the tomatoes at very good prices that we had never received before. I got enough money and bought a dairy cow that is producing milk now for the family use. My parents-in-law were bothering me about paying them dowry. So I used some of the money from the tomato sales to buy cattle at good prices through *Soko Hewani* also and paid the dowry. Now my parents-in-law don't bother me anymore; they are happy with me and I am staying with my wife in peace.

The call center operates 24/7 and can handle thirty calls at a time. During the day it is manned by live operators called agents. At night and during holidays, the calls are automatically recorded; they are attended to the first thing the next day. Buying and selling bids and other offers are entered in a database that is accessible to all callers. For example, somebody can call and say they would like to buy a dairy cow. The agent goes to the database to see if someone has made such an offer to sell and how many, how much, and where. To sustain operations, KACE has added two additional services to provide revenue streams. For a small prenegotiated commission, KACE staff can broker the deal for the seller and buyer. And they have negotiated with the phone companies so that when someone calls the center, KACE gets a percentage of the airtime revenues.

All four information dissemination platforms are designed to serve all the actors in the agriculture chain—from the least sophisticated to the most.

> So our target client is a smaller illiterate farmer. We want to improve his livelihood. But to develop markets for farmers, we cannot just focus on farmers, we have to involve everyone from the farmer to the buyer to the consumer or processor along the way. That's why we developed a market information and linkage system that is looking at the whole continuum of the value chain.

The Rebirth of Farming and Farmers

KACE is catching on. Each month about eight hundred people visit the centers for information; fifty thousand a month come through the SMS service; fifteen thousand from the website and two thousand through the interactive voice messaging. Adrian estimates that 5 million listeners tune in to *Soko Hewani* every week.

Interestingly enough there are about six hundred KACE users who receive information daily, sent from the electronic database, many of them residing outside Kenya—in America, Europe, Southeast Asia, and South Africa. The number of people who use all these channels is consistently increasing every month.

But most important, with this new source of information, farmers are starting to make money and realize more profits. They are more organized, efficient and empowered. Rural farmers are beginning to see themselves as being able to build a better life for their families, and a younger generation is noticing and beginning to consider agriculture as a way to gain a better livelihood than they previously thought possible.

As Africa's economy grows at about 5 percent a year, it is seeing the rise of a middle class with more money in their pockets and an appetite for better food and higher-value products. A demand and an opportunity is being created like none before, and farmers in Kenya—and, all over Africa—not only need to use market information more skillfully, they also need to harness technology and the skills of the younger educated population to improve agricultural productivity and support economic growth and livelihood improvement. For this reason, Adrian has started to partner with the International Livestock Research Institute in Kenya to develop a dairy industry not just in that country but throughout East Africa.

Suddenly there's a demand for improved heifers by young farmers who are going into the dairy business.

> *But they don't know where to get the heifers, or some of those who are breeders, they don't know where to sell this demand. So we're developing a platform through the market call center and* Soko Hewani *that targets the dairy industry and helps people market and improve their breeds.*

Adrian's work is clearly changing the model of agriculture from subsistence to commercialization, from illiterate older farmers to educated younger people who see that with improved markets, there is a business to be made, there is a livelihood to be earned from farming. There is an agricultural evolution going on in Africa, and Adrian is in the center of the upward spiral.

Though KACE's information is now helping to grow markets in and outside of Kenya, currently Africa trades more with the outside world than within itself. Adrian's vision is to see Africa create large internal trading blocs so that they create markets that serve the 1 billion indigenous Africans. KACE would expand to improve efficiencies of market systems and build the foundation for promoting not just Kenyan but also inter-regional trade within Africa as well as extra-Africa international trade. Clearly Adrian is already starting to prepare and equip the next generation of farmers for the challenge.

CHAPTER 7

Stimulating Fiscal Vibrancy by Creating a New Economy—Brazil

Joaquim de Melo Neto is the founder of Banco Palmas, referred to as "the People's Bank." It is Brazil's first community development bank. Using its own alternative currency (called "Palmas") the bank operates within the community to stimulate growth and economic opportunity.

PICTURE YOURSELF APPLYING FOR A LOAN TO BUY A HOUSE JUST A few streets away from where you work. The bank's loan officers investigate your credit history, so they know there is a good chance that you will be able to repay. Soon you will live in a new house close to your place of business. You won't have to commute every day, so you can sell your car and save money by doing so. You can buy everything you need: food, clothes, shoes, and medicines in the neighborhood. Your children can walk to the nearby school. You will end up spending most of your income in your new neighborhood and your neighbors will probably do the same. The local shops will prosper, the schools will hire more teachers, the food market will need to expand its business, and your bank and service industries will be there to support you and your neighbors while they turn a profit. Life is good.

Then picture yourself as part of an impoverished community, where most people do not have formal nine-to-five jobs. Because the community does not support many employment opportunities, when you do go to work, it's usually outside the community. Because the community is very poor, there's no reason for a bank to open an office—there isn't enough business to sustain it. Without a bank, you and your neighbors have no access to legal credit—you can't buy a house; you can't start businesses. There is no support for shops, schools, or markets. As a result, whatever money you have, you have no choice but to spend it elsewhere—outside the community. With not much being spent or sold in the area, no local economy is generated and the cycle of poverty perpetuates itself. You and the residents of your community remain underserved and poor. Life is not so good; in fact, it's pretty bleak.

A Self-Sustaining Slum?

In the 1970s, Brazil was under a severe dictatorship and any kind of political action was prohibited. A new movement called Liberation Theology, which connected Christian theology and political activism, was growing fast in Latin America and serving as a pathway for several priests to get engaged with underserved communities. Joaquim de Melo Neto was one of them. While he was training to become a priest, Joaquim started to work in very poor communities, ones which were completely out of the mainstream and forgotten by the government. It was then he decided that if he could find ways to help those communities access their rights so they could raise their standard of living and improve their situation, he would spend his life doing so.

When he moved to the Conjunto Palmeiras, a slum on the outskirts of Fortaleza (in northeast Brazil), Joaquim realized that the absence of any infrastructure in the area and the distressed economic conditions of the people would require more than just a small group of committed citizens fighting for their rights. He needed to gather and engage the support of the entire community to help them build the type of environment they wanted for themselves. He organized the slum into groups of local stakeholders: people affiliated with the churches, those active in the schools, the soccer clubs, the cultural groups. All of them came together to create an association, which had the responsibility of building a new neighborhood—more organized and integrated, designed with the needs of the residents in mind. Almost immediately, the association decided it needed to develop a community center to train local people on how to defend their own rights. The training led to the beginning of a new dialogue with the local government—one that would later support the implementation of public policies around sanitation, electricity use, and transportation in the slum, and would prove to benefit underserved communities all over Brazil.

However, after many long and hard years working to improve Conjunto Palmeiras, Joaquim started to notice that the poor economy and the lack of nearby jobs had families migrating away from the area. It was then he realized that to enable the community to flourish to the point where it could sustain itself, it needed not only a local infrastructure and improved conditions but also new opportunities for local people. A short time later, the idea of creating a "bank of and for the people"—to stimulate and facilitate the local economy—came into being.

Could Just Anyone Create a Bank?

In the late 1990s, Joaquim and the Neighborhood Association of Conjunto Palmeiras created the *Banco Palmas* (Palmas Bank), which was operated and managed entirely by community leaders as a people's bank. The bank's core philosophy involved a balance between production and consumption. Its purpose was to encourage and incentivize the growth of a network of producers and consumers inside the community so the residents could produce and purchase much of what they needed from each other, through their local initiatives. The people's bank developed a line of microcredit for those wishing to create or expand small businesses and another line of credit for those who wished to purchase products from the neighborhood. In this way the buying and selling of products from small merchants and producers within the community was facilitated, circulating incomes within the neighborhood and thereby promoting economic growth.

For the network to function, Joaquim had to establish alternative instruments and tools for local consumption (vouchers that would work like credit cards), alternative sales outlets (street fairs, farmers' markets, and small stores), and a specific code of conduct that encouraged residents to adopt a culture of cooperation. Producers were encouraged to form a "solidarity network," where they all would agree to purchase from each other. The broom-maker would sell brooms to the neighborhood's tailor, who in turn sells dresses to the broom-maker. Obviously, the chain of products and transactions gets longer and more sophisticated as more and more residents participate in the exchanges.

The retail stores were also encouraged to purchase products that were produced in the community and offer them for sale to the local population, who would now be doing their shopping in the neighborhood stores. This dynamic created a virtuous circle where those who produce can sell; the more they sell the more jobs are created, the more residents are working, the more purchases are made. In the end, economic development outperforms poverty.

To make this cycle self-sustaining, Joaquim knew that he would have to find a way to guarantee income, as well as a way to keep that income in the community. The community-owned Palmas Bank decided to create its own currency, called "Palmas," that would be recognized as money but that stayed within the community as an alternative for the official Brazilian currency. The Palmas money was quickly adopted, accepted, and recognized by local producers, merchants, and consumers. There was a huge effort to engage everyone in using Palmas, which started to circulate daily between the local shops and people, facilitating businesses, generating local wealth, creating solidarity and an alternative market among the families. As Joaquim explains: "This generated a great self-disciplining trust among the residents for a system that they themselves created."

Solidarity Economics

Joaquim insists that the entire conception of the Palmas Bank—from the initial strategies to the management of the resources—was carried out by the community itself. The first thing the community did was to map the local production and consumption in the neighborhood and survey the inputs used in production. The survey results identified the sites where producers and consumers were making their purchases and provided a clear picture of what needed to be produced, where, by whom, the resources available, and the resources needed. With this information, the community again got together to decide the operating model for the bank. For Joaquim, community management is the "wellspring of empowerment"—the place from which the community derives its nourishment so it can increase its capacity, develop its technical abilities, and grow its skills in negotiating with governments.

Palmas Bank was conceived as an integrated system, making loans for production and also lending to local consumers. It therefore helps stores find markets for products, it offers professional training in the strategy of solidarity economics, it develops incubators to reintegrate women into production, and it conducts a range of activities that support the production chain as a whole: including solidarity capital, sustainable production, fair trade, and ethical consumption. Joaquim believes that the poor can only have the opportunity for social inclusion and local development if all these aspects are addressed simultaneously.

When I first read about Joaquim's work, it was hard to understand how a person who was most interested in becoming a priest could create a new economy. It occurred to me that the work he did when he was studying to be a priest taught him about community organizing and how to understand the environment and the needs of the residents among whom he lived. He knew how to listen and how to empathize, and he built a financial institution based on those principles—created with, by, and for the people he was motivated to help.

Decentralize the Model, Develop a Movement

In the first few months of operation, Banco Palmas was able to prove its worth to the local community. But to succeed at a more substantial level, it had to expand its sphere of influence outside the community. It managed to do just that, and was becoming so successful that in its first year, the federal government, through the Central Bank of Brazil, began to get uncomfortable with the idea that Joaquim was creating a parallel system of currency that could have negative implications for the Brazilian economy. Slowly and patiently, Joaquim proved to the government that the Banco Palmas model was the best way to develop the depressed communities that existed throughout Brazil.

By using testimony of people whose lives and livelihoods were being changed by the bank, Joaquim convinced the government critics that he was not trying to replace the Brazilian currency; he was just developing good mechanisms to empower local communities to develop themselves. As Elias Lino—bank member, beneficiary, and changemaker—observes:

> A community bank is one of the few ways in which the marginalized people like me can change or improve collectively. In other words, while the local and global economy provide few opportunities for the poor, organizations like Banco Palmas show that by creating the right environment, anyone can be included in changing their destiny.

Joaquim's arguments and examples were so effective that not long after, the Brazilian Central Bank created an official department to monitor the creation of other community banks and the spread of the Banco Palmas model in the country.

Six years after Banco Palmas was created, a second community bank came into being in the Brazilian state of Ceará. After that, many other local organizations created their own banks. Now, there are sixty-three "community development banks," as they are called, in twelve states of Brazil. They all belong to a national network created to define and enhance the common work methods they use.

Beyond Banking

According to the Instituto de Pesquisa Econômica Aplicada, in January 2011, 39.5 percent of the Brazilian population did not have access to capital via a bank account. In the Northeast region of the country (where Banco Palmas is located) it is 52.6 percent. Traditional banks were never interested in opening branches in small and poor neighborhoods, so a partnership with a community development bank represented a great opportunity for forward-thinking banks and other institutions to step into a new line of business. As an example, Banco Popular do Brasil became a partner of the community banks as a guarantor of credit lines. At the same time, community banks became agents of Banco Popular do Brasil, allowing the communities to make and receive payments like pension benefits, operate checking and savings accounts, and enjoy other banking services. It became a win-win situation for everyone involved: the community, Banco Palmas, and Banco Popular do Brasil.

Banco Palmas was the first program that Joaquim created under his official organization, Instituto Palmas. Operating at the macro level, Instituto Palmas is responsible for gathering data about what the banks are doing and releasing publications about the outcome, the issues that affect the banks, and examples of solutions that some of the banks are implementing. This information supports the existing banks with important data and current trends and assists in the formation of new local banks. To sustain and grow the community bank concept while increasing its value to all its investors and partners, Instituto Palmas also provides a six-hundred-hour course to train local people across the country to negotiate and manage financial partnerships, develop new financial products and services, and disseminate the model. Recently, it partnered with three top universities in Brazil to help local communities create and implement their own banks.

All of Instituto Palmas's work is focused on propelling traditionally marginalized communities into fiscal vibrancy by supporting and encouraging economic growth. Joaquim is now playing a key role in developing an array of new financial products as well as technological services for the banks. A partnership with Zurich Financial Services developed a new line of insurance products; a partnership with Mahiti Infotech, a software firm in India (run by another Ashoka Fellow), is developing the "Free and Open Source Software Platform" for management of networks of community banks along with a mobile banking application. Indeed, keeping up with technologic advances is one of the most important challenges Instituto Palmas faces. In the meantime, Joaquim has identified many other opportunities and sees the work of Instituto Palmas expanding in the coming years—always in "true and open partnerships" with local communities and private and public institutions.

The Key to Financial Inclusion

Joaquim used to think that the financial system is something very distant and too complex for the poor. He himself couldn't understand how it worked. When he first understood the need to develop a local economy, he knew that he had to learn how this sector operated and try to demystify it to the poor. In these last years, he has realized that it is not as complicated as he thought. The hard part was to convince the banks and the government that poor people could also qualify for credit and be included financially. If this happened, then it was possible to change the dynamics of the existing economic scenario in slums and for slum dwellers. He just needed to create a financial and economic mechanism that made sense according to the reality of the community.

Traditional banks know that they have a long way to go in terms of learning how communities think and behave. Perhaps that's the reason that even institutions like regular banks now realize that if they really want to include everyone, they have to re-create their own operational systems. To do that, they are taking a serious look at the components of the community development banks that make them successful and profitable. For example, among other things, each community development bank is charged with stimulating the creation of local production and consumption and supporting all the businesses in the community. Most important, each is owned and managed by the community itself. Joaquim can already envision the impact on communities all over the world, if more traditional banks could incorporate some of these elements in their existing models, as did Banco Popular do Brasil. Since he firmly believes that financial inclusion is only possible when the poor are socially and productively included, he knows that is the key to success that banks can use to open their doors to everyone.

Using Market Forces to Create Social Value

This section explores three innovative ways of bringing the business and social sectors together to create sustainable partnerships that tackle huge social problems impacting large numbers of people. Far different from corporate social responsibility (CSR) programs, these partnerships create a hybrid adaptation that establishes a profitable business for the sole (soul) purpose of supporting, fueling growth, and sustaining a social purpose.

Profit is not a dirty word—if profits are recycled back into the business or used to sustain or increase employment or wages and provide access to opportunities for those who are marginalized, impoverished, or in temporary need. In many cases, profits placed somewhere in the project's trajectory can augment the impact and provide incentives for sustainability. For example, DMT Mobile Toilets creates employment, livelihood, and ownership with profits generated from the pay-for-use model; Chenelet uses a for-profit paper pallet business as a base for generating a public eco-housing enterprise; Ciudad Saludable creates micro-enterprises out of garbage collection. They are all examples of triple-bottom-line missions that provide measurable impact from extracting the social value in market forces. They are all part of the evolving "business social sector."

REFLECTIONS BY
WILLIAM JEFFERSON CLINTON

In the ten years since I started the Clinton Foundation, the world has become more interdependent than ever. Successful countries need not only a vigorous private sector and an effective government but also innovative nongovernmental groups that can bridge the gap between what the private sector can produce and the government can provide. At their best, nongovernmental groups work with the private sector and government to solve problems and seize opportunities faster, at lower cost, and with greater impact than any sector could acting alone. Social entrepreneurs are in a unique position to reduce the drastic inequalities and instabilities that undermine the promise of our interdependent world.

We started the Clinton Global Initiative to create these kinds of partnerships between world leaders, business executives, and innovative nongovernmental groups to solve some of the world's most pressing issues. CGI members make Commitments to Action—concrete, measurable steps toward improving lives that rely on sustainable, market-based solutions. As of 2011, CGI partnerships have already improved the lives of 300 million people in more than 180 countries and are valued in excess of $63 billion.

In 2009, a commitment made through CGI launched a program that lets Nigerian patients identify counterfeit prescription drugs using their cell phones. In a country where 80 percent of drugs are corrupted, patients can now text a code found on their prescription bottle and receive an authenticity report directly from the company, Sproxil. Today, this technology has been used more than a hundred thousand times, and with the support of the Nigeria Food and Drug authority, Sproxil has agreed to expand its efforts to protect a million more patients in the developing world while simultaneously supporting the legitimate pharmaceutical companies who produce the medicine.

As our worldwide initiatives foster partnerships between private enterprise and social ventures, fresh, innovative approaches are often the keys to success. In Peru and Colombia, the Clinton Giustra Sustainable Growth Initiative developed a web-based system to keep in constant touch with all aspects of its various development projects, including successful new collaborations between small suppliers and hotels in Cartagena. By creating a monitoring system that is accessible on computers, smart phones, and tablets, we no longer have to wait until a program ends to analyze results; we're able to expand what's working and correct what isn't while the work is in progress.

In Seoul, South Korea, the Clinton Climate Initiative is working with a housing contractor on an 830-acre development whose emissions will be roughly 80 percent below typical current levels. The venture will create a district heating and cooling facility powered largely by sewer heat, and build a fuel cell–based combined heat and power plant that will provide up to 20 megawatts of power.

If we are to build an interdependent world of shared opportunities, shared prosperity, and shared responsibilities—one where we celebrate our differences but affirm the primary importance of our common humanity—we will rely even more heavily on strategies that are sustainable, replicable, and measurable. Government, the private sector, and NGOs must continue working together to find innovative ways to keep widening the circle of opportunity and responsibility.

William Jefferson Clinton served as the 42nd president of the United States (1993–2001). In 2001 Clinton established the William J. Clinton Foundation to promote and address international causes such as the prevention of AIDS and global warming.

CHAPTER 8

From Garbage to Gold — Peru

Albina Ruiz is building a community-based solid waste management system that plays an increasingly important role in improving sanitation and health conditions in Peru and other countries in Latin America. Every stage of the waste management cycle creates a network of employment and income-generating enterprises that integrates business and social value throughout the entire process.

Every time I go to a waste dump, whether it is in Brazil, Colombia, Guatemala, Peru, or India, my heart breaks when I see human beings like you and me, who are working, many accompanied by their children, in deplorable risky conditions. Their working and living conditions encourage me to work tirelessly and try to change this situation. I envision a world where millions of waste pickers become part of the formal waste management system with strong support of the public/private sector and civil society.

—ALBINA RUIZ

IT WAS 1986. A PETITE, DARK-HAIRED TWENTY-EIGHT-YEAR-OLD spitfire of a woman stood up before an angry, raucous crowd of more than six hundred men at a Union of Municipal Workers meeting on the outskirts of Lima a few months after she'd been hired as the first female director of the municipality. The union workers were about to demand her resignation. Hardly a surprise, as much to the annoyance of the union workers, the woman who angered them had just spent the first few months in her position trying to weed out the corruption that surrounded public garbage collections, and she was about to design a new system for trash collection that would extend into the poorest sections of Lima.

Albina Ruiz was, by her own account, almost obsessed with the trash that seemed to overwhelm Lima. Since moving there she had been shocked and dismayed at the condition of the streets. The heaps of rubbish in many parts of the city were so massive that they stopped growing vertically and were now spreading horizontally like algae, covering anything in their path. Garbage was all around, so people tossed trash everywhere—in the streets, rivers, and vacant lots, creating a perpetually nasty environment that many residents found dispiriting. The downward spiral was palpable everywhere she looked.

109

No one was picking up the garbage in these parts of the city because the poor couldn't pay and the city believed (as one municipal official told me) that poor people liked to be dirty.

Trying to change the existing collection system and develop a new one gave Albina a *huge* problem with the union, which liked things just the way they were and had no incentive to change anything. It was no coincidence that the first item on the union meeting agenda was asking for Albina's resignation. But when the vote came up, no one was prepared to see her stand up and say, "If there is someone else in the hall who is more able to run this municipality than me I will gladly give them my position." The entire room fell silent. Everyone was so dumbfounded that they stood for a long few moments without saying a word, and hardly taking a collective breath. No one stood up to claim the position, and the voting item was permanently removed from the agenda.

Trash Talk

Only one year prior to the meeting, Albina had received her engineering degree, and her outspokenness and passionate belief that Peru could control its garbage problem garnered the attention of the mayor of the nearby municipality of El Agustino. Luckily he was not one of the Lima mayors who had inaugurated the "public improvement program" to build ramps from the streets to the river so people could dump their garbage directly into the water! Fortunately, this mayor was able to understand Albina's vision of using garbage as a medium for addressing a deeper issue that plagued his municipality.

Albina realized that garbage represented people. For every piece of discarded material there is a person behind it and in front of it. Where many see trash as a problem, she saw an opportunity. An opportunity to give jobs, an opportunity to improve the environment, an opportunity to improve public health, an opportunity to create more social entrepreneurs, along with political and business entrepreneurs. She believed that each sector of society could not accomplish its own roles effectively without depending on the others. Her vision soared way above all the mounds of garbage put together:

> *We depend on the business sector and we also depend on the State. We need enterprising businessmen and women (which there are more and more of) and we also need enterprising civil servants and enterprising public authorities who are also thinking how they can fulfill their role as a civil authority and be political in diverse and creative ways. And I think that when those three sectors come together then we are really talking about shaping our city, changing the world, and being different.*

From Pit to Potential

Albina's words are even more visionary when you consider that she was born—and lived up until high school graduation—in the Peruvian jungle. Her words are even more amazing when you consider that she was a farmers' daughter who not only finished high school but was inspired to become an engineer. It was Peru's luck that there was no university for her to study engineering in the rainforest, so she had to move to Lima to fulfill her educational goals.

She came to Lima excited to experience big city life, but much to her disappointment when she got there all she could focus on was the mountains of smelly and insect-infected garbage piled in the streets. Nowhere had she seen garbage like that, for in the jungle everything that was discarded by one person was useful in some way to someone or something else. Moreover, the garbage issue was inescapable—when she moved to Lima in 1983 the city only picked up one-third of the more than 3,500 metric tons of daily garbage, resulting in trash being strewn over the other two-thirds of Lima. In the poorest areas, the ones the city ignored and where private garbage associations did not even bother to intervene, some streets looked like open-sky dumps and the air was foul and unbreathable. To Albina the situation was a huge disappointment, not at all how she had envisioned big city life to be. From where she lived, Lima looked and smelled like one big garbage pit.

This sense of incongruity never left her, so when she was about to graduate as an engineer she decided to focus one of her course assignments on measuring the efficiency of garbage truck pickups and developed a plan for optimization of pickup routes. While her classmates were analyzing supermarkets and banks, she was all about garbage. Always in the back of her mind she was trying to answer her one big question: *Why wasn't the garbage getting picked up where I lived?* The obvious answer, realized as a result of her now-completed course assignment, was that the city trucks were physically too big to go around the piles of garbage in the streets and to travel up the narrow, hilly roads that skirted the downtown where the largest proportion of the poor lived. It was then that it struck her—a new system needed to be developed.

Garbage as a Useable Asset

When she could literally and figuratively see beyond the garbage she noticed the huge number of people who lived off of it—the garbage pickers and recyclers. There were the *porcicultores*, who fed pigs from the organic discards; the *cochineros*, who collected iron scraps and bottles; and the assorted recyclers who opened the bags of trash and hauled away cardboard, paper, plastic, and anything else that they could use. These people had descriptive names but little dignity and almost no income, and they were living very hazardous lives in disease-infested surroundings. These people would be the ones Albina would organize into an association of recyclers, an association that encouraged a culture of paid garbage collection in the poorest sections of the city, helped cultivate a household practice of garbage separation into recyclables, and inculcated a philosophy of garbage as a usable asset—which preceded a decrease in the practice of dumping garbage everywhere. These were the people Albina inspired to be changemakers—people who would help themselves, their families, and their neighbors, and turn the garbage of Lima into gold.

Albina set about designing and building a new type of small tricycle truck that could fit through the narrow, hilly streets and around the garbage that blocked the roads. She started to envision a system interweaving community tricycle collection trucks, garbage collectors, and waste recycling, partnered with a public campaign that would convince people to wait for the trucks to throw their garbage out. This dream would all be predicated on a small monthly household payment that the residents of the slums would pay for the services. But new systems that replace or circumvent the old ones necessarily involve changes, and change always creates obstacles that need to be surmounted; obstacles causing friction, belligerence, envy, jealously—even violence. But Albina already intuitively knew that her role would always involve some greater or smaller level of risk to herself as the person who attempts to create the changes in the first place. She was prepared to take that risk.

Fast Forward 2010

For more than twenty-five years Albina has been working in waste management, and since early this century, she has been the founder and director of Ciudad Saludable, an NGO that is building a community-based solid waste management system and playing an increasingly important role in improving sanitation and health conditions not only in Lima but around Peru and other areas of Latin America. The centerpiece of her strategy is an inclusive and highly networked system of community-organized and effectively linked collection, recycling, and disposal activities. Included are related initiatives to control illegal dumping and eliminate illegal dump sites. Her primary tool is employment, and she uses it by organizing the recyclers into income-generating micro-enterprises, a strategy built into every stage of the waste management cycle.

These micro-enterprises are structured into quasi-independent and self-sustaining organizations that assure both the efficiency of the overall operation and widespread community participation in the planning, execution, evaluation, and fine-tuning of the endeavor. From her initial effort to coordinate an illegal underground economy of slum-dwelling garbage pickers into an association of recyclers, she has consistently added each successive piece into her mental blueprint in order to make system change possible. She worked to promote the first law on solid wastes that addressed recycling and reusing as well as recognizing the recyclers as a legitimate part of the process and, after twenty years of persistence, witnessed the passage of that law by an act of Peru's Congress. Like a mother hen, she nurtured the establishment of hundreds of trash and recycling micro-enterprises after she initiated a credit fund for recyclers so they could set up services in their communities and use the money to buy, use, and make products from the recycled materials.

Albina has developed an innovative chain of employment and income-generating micro-enterprises, enabling an entire new classification of changemakers to emerge. These changemakers themselves become community micro-entrepreneurs—who start small businesses that take charge of collecting and processing the garbage. They take advantage of the microloans Ciudad Saludable makes available to them and in turn hire others as employees to work alongside, expanding the employment pool and creating virtuous cycles of change that positively impact their families, friends, neighbors, community, and city.

From Local Ideas to Lasting Solutions

Sonia Quispe makes handicrafts and purses from the recyclable materials generated by Ciudad Saludable. She is the manager of Ecomanos, a micro-enterprise where she employs six women who transform recyclable material into wallets, purses, picture frames, and other items that are sold in high-end stores. She also leads workshops on handicraft production in schools.

> Ciudad Saludable and Albina Ruiz have transformed my life from a waste picker, who used to collect organic material to feed pigs, to an entrepreneur who can support her family and even send one of my children to college. The children in my workshop in school actually address me as "teacher." My life has changed radically and I am aware that I have become a role model to others.

Today Albina oversees collection and recycling projects in twenty cities across Peru, employs more than 150 people, and serves over 3 million residents. Ciudad Saludable's approach to waste management is so successful that she has been asked to come up with a national plan for Peru, while other Latin American countries have expressed interest in emulating her method. She has developed and built an incredible organization that came from an unlikely beginning. She chose to enlist the outcasts of the community—those who sift through garbage dumps daily in order to find something to live on—and provide them official employment, health care, and clean work uniforms. She organized recycling and waste collection, negotiated trades, worked with banks and businesspeople to build sustainability into her model, and partnered with the city in many of these endeavors.

Now she is building an even bigger client base for the recyclers by helping urban pig and goat farmers increase their effectiveness so they can become economically viable. In turn, they will increase their use of discarded organic matter and create yet another new market for the recyclers. By all measures, Ciudad Saludable has achieved enormous success. By working in teams, rubbish collectors gather more waste each day, make more trades, and make a better living. With the merit and importance of sustainability in the community recognized by people around them, the collectors and recyclers now carry themselves with pride and consider themselves micro-business owners or employees. Helping people regain and retain their human dignity is a gamechanger and dignity is something that is usually passed on to others. It is close to infectious. These are the ways lives get transformed and in turn they transform others around them. Says Nelly Ticse, a former waste picker and now member of the RUPA Association of Recyclers in San Juan de Miraflores District:

> Before, I was not able to speak up or look into the eyes when talking to someone because I was embarrassed and afraid of people who used to insult and call us demeaning names. However, after Ciudad Saludable transformed my job from a waste picker to a recycler, now I know that what I do is worth it and that we add value to society, the environment, and even the economy of Peru. Today, I speak up loudly and I make sure people respect my work. I am not afraid to speak with the mayor of my city, the senators in the Congress, and journalists because I learned to convey my ideas and the recyclers' dreams. Now people have a lot of respect for our work.

As Peru Changes, So Can the World

As for the future, Albina will continue moving forward. Her vision is to make sure that Peru is no longer a huge garbage can, but rather that Peru becomes a clean country, a sound country, a healthy country. Her plans, however, are far bigger than Peru and extend to Latin America, India, and Africa.

> *In Peru we have demonstrated that we can have a law. In Peru, we have demonstrated that the president of the Republic has received the recyclers in the government palace. That the minister of environment has meetings with them, and that the vice minister sits with them every week to work on regulations. We have demonstrated this. If we have done this in Peru then we can do it in any other country—wherever there is a need and wherever there are people who are as concerned with others as they are with themselves. Wherever there are people who pride themselves in being changemakers. Because in reality the people know that they can change.*

Albina's daughter, Paloma, who also works at Ciudad Saludable as director of education, bears testament to the spirit that Albina is instilling in everyone who surrounds her:

> I think of the people I grew up with, one is a single mom, the other married to a delinquent. Why am I different? It is the living example of my parents. With education, with love, with all this pride in yourself and your family, life can be completely different. I have asked myself if I am ready to make these sacrifices that call for service to make a change in the world. I look at my parents and see the love they have for changing things for others and see that they made it themselves. I know I can too. It is a very lovely thing.

117

In the end, one wonders if Albina's ultimate vision is to bring the wisdom of her childhood education in the jungle to the rest of the world. Value everything, use all, know that something of no value to you has value to someone or something else, leave no footprint, involve the entire village, consider your relationship to everyone and everything.

Maybe we could use a little more jungle within us all.

CHAPTER 9

A Better Model of Capitalism—United States

Paul Rice is the founder, president, and CEO of FairTrade USA, the leading third-party certifier of Fair Trade products in the United States. The organization's mission is to enable sustainable development and community empowerment and to cultivate a more equitable global trade model that benefits farmers, workers, consumers, industry, and the earth.

You know, there's a poverty statistic that sears my brain:
2 billion people on this planet live on $2 a day. I've lived in the
global south long enough to know that even on a diet of rice,
beans, and tortillas three times a day, $2 is not enough to eat.
So in the pale of things, the 1.4 million families representing
8 million people that Fair Trade serves in the global south is just
a start. It's a good start, but it's just a start. The model that we
are using will need to go from 1 million farmers to 100 million,
which is the aspiration. And then from 100 million to 1 billion.
Scale for me looks like that. And the day that I discover that
Fair Trade can't do that is the day that I leave to be a part of the
next great innovation. I'm still here because I still believe that
the core principles of this model are scalable and are capable of
attaining that billion people mark in the future.

—PAUL RICE

PAUL RICE WAS BROUGHT UP BY "WONDER WOMAN": A SINGLE
mother who was raised on a farm in the Depression and orphaned
by age twelve. She knew what it was to go to bed without
supper—and though Paul thankfully did not, he grew up with
stories about life on the farm and what it meant to work hard
and still not be able to put food on the table. He always felt his
connection to hard-working farming folk. As a kid and a young
adult, he had this sense of outrage and indignation at poverty, at
hunger, at injustice, at this very notion of people going without in
a world of plenty.

He started to question the root causes of hunger and poverty
and puzzled over why hunger exists in countries that are net
exporters of food. Was it because of unfair land distribution, lack
of access to capital, or other things that needed to be in place in
order to produce enough food to decrease poverty, or something
else? And so, in that mind space—a university student's activist
indignation about the powers that be and compassion for the

downtrodden—he decided that he had to go and do something about it.

Simultaneously, Nicaragua was in the midst of a revolution, and by taking land from the rich and giving it to the poor, it seemed to Paul to be addressing some of the structural root causes of poverty. It all matched Paul's sentiments, so in the summer of 1983 he bought a one-way ticket to Nicaragua and went off to join the revolution. His goal was to work alongside impoverished farmers in the developing world, get some field experience, stay for a couple of years, and then figure out what to do with the rest of his life. He ended up staying for eleven years.

What Can't Be Done, Must Be Done

Paul's first seven years were, by his account, spent in a series of failed programs. And those programs were very much characteristic of the dominant model of poverty alleviation that the international aid community had implemented since World War II. Very top-down, driven by well-intentioned people sitting in offices in Washington, London, and Paris and sending millions of aid dollars to the global south. More often than not as Paul worked on those projects, he felt that what they were creating was dependency on aid. They did not help people in the villages develop their own capacity to solve their own problems.

Much of this failure, Paul observed, was rooted in the singular focus of most aid programs on production. These programs tried to teach farmers how to double their yields on a given acre of land by using agrochemicals and hybrid seeds. Yet even when farmers succeeded in producing more on their land, the production costs of chemical-intensive agriculture were often so high that farmers went into debt as a result. In the end, Paul came to believe that raising families out of poverty didn't just depend on how much corn or coffee the farmers were taught to produce. It was about the price they sold those harvests for at the end of the season. The farmers were no better off because they lacked direct access to the market and were forced to sell their harvests to local middlemen at extremely low prices. By ignoring the marketplace, the development projects Paul worked on ultimately failed to help farmers lift themselves out of poverty.

Trade, Not Aid

As Paul started to think more about production and pricing dilemmas, he heard about groups in Europe calling themselves "Fair Traders" who were interested in promoting economic and environmental sustainable development along with poverty alleviation not through aid but through more equitable trade. The notion was that if you paid farmers a better price for their hard work and their harvest, they could elevate their standards of living through their own efforts rather than through international charity.

Taking a page from the organic certification movement, Paul found a European buyer who was willing to pay more than ten times the current Nicaraguan price per kilo for quality coffee. Because there was no cash to pay the farmers for the first shipment, each had to be convinced to deliver ten sacks of coffee on consignment, so that they could fill and ship a container-load of coffee. After months of traveling around the countryside, meeting with farmers he had known and worked with for many years, Paul was only able to recruit twenty-four brave souls to take this leap of faith. It usually took these one- and two-acre farm families an entire year to produce an average of 2,000 pounds of coffee (a ton). At the going rate of ten cents a pound, they would have earned just $200 for an entire year's work. Not even a dollar a day.

But because Paul had united them in this singular effort, they were, together, able to fill a container of coffee to ship overseas. Three months later, Paul called a meeting in a schoolhouse in Santo Domingo, and everyone—the farmers, their wives, the kids, the grandmas, and even their dogs—came to see what he had done with their coffee. Paul had a tackle box full of cash; they had netted $1 per pound. Instead of the $200 they could have hoped to earn for the year, they were now being paid $2,000 on average. It was more money than most of these people had ever seen in their lives. Overnight, Paul became a legend and his nickname became "Pablo un dollar."

By the second year, 350 families signed up, and by the third year there were 3,000, all in the Segovias region of northern Nicaragua. Thanks to Paul, the families now milled their coffee as a group and then exported it direct, jumping over three different levels of middlemen and capturing that value for themselves. This was the start of the first Fair Trade certified cooperative in Nicaragua—Prodecoop—in 1990.

From Good Intentions to Positive Change

The cultural and political significance of the cooperative was extraordinary. These small farmers grew coffee not because it was a business but because their granddaddies and great-granddaddies had grown coffee. Their very identity was steeped in coffee production. And that's all they could imagine for themselves, ever. Now they were learning to wear multiple hats in order to control costs and increase their profits. They learned to mill, truck, and export. Eventually, they learned to be bankers as well, because along with their success, they needed to set up village banks to manage the new money coming into the communities. To reduce dependence on expensive and environmentally destructive chemicals they set up an organic training and certification program for their members. The communities started building schools. They started drilling wells to bring in clean drinking water for the first time. All the things that the villagers had passively waited for government or charities to do, they were now doing for themselves. The invisible dividend that surrounded all this growth was the pride and dignity they gained by doing it for themselves, with no one's handout subsidizing that journey. As Paul came to realize,

Empowerment is an overused term. It's a cliché. And yet it's as tangible and real and noticeable as talking to a farmer and having that farmer look you in the eye instead of looking at the ground, hat in hand, when he talks to you as a foreigner.

Two years after Prodecoop was formed, its success influenced the creation of another nearby cooperative, Aldea Global (Asociación Aldea Global Jinotega). It was founded by twenty-two indigenous farmers in the mountainous region of northern Nicaragua to promote sustainable agricultural practices that would help protect their environment and improve their quality of life.

Today, with 1,200 members, the association focuses on the growth of the cooperative by promoting efficient commercialization, solidarity, and alternative credit services, while maintaining a commitment to the environment. It has also made gender equity a priority. Earning Fair Trade certification from Fairtrade Labelling Organizations International in 2004 has helped achieve those goals. In addition, it was awarded the "2007 Global Vision Award: Community Outreach" by *Travel + Leisure Magazine*. In the same

The impact of FairTrade doesn't just refer to the possibility for a family to earn more from their harvest, but rather through the organization, they become the protagonist in their own development. FairTrade offers us the opportunities with which we can positively influence the construction of a more equitable society.

—RUFINO HERRERA PUELLO, ASOCIACIÓN ALDEA GLOBAL JINOTEGA

year, the cooperative was awarded the "Best Associative Company" of the year by the Association of Producers and Exporters of Nicaragua. Aldea Global is illustrative of the growth of cooperatives throughout the country and the far-reaching impact of the Fair Trade movement on thousands of farmers, their families, their villages, and their future.

Paul found this journey of market-based empowerment and sustainable development so transformational that he was inspired to stay in Nicaragua and grow the coffee business he started. But ultimately, his success was what inspired him to come back to the United States:

After four years of running Prodecoop and seeing this dramatic transformation in literally hundreds of villages and thousands of families all over northern Nicaragua, I realized how transformational it was. This is a better model for sustainable development and community empowerment than anything I had ever worked on before or anything the major agencies are working on. Europe

*was leading the way, and America was hardly dipping its toe in
the water. To be sure, there were a few small fair trade businesses
capturing a few million dollars of business a year, but that was out
of an $18 billion coffee market which 30 million farmers around
the world supply. They hardly made a dent. I asked myself, why
isn't anyone in the U.S. stepping up and replicating, or translating or reinventing the European experience so that it's relevant
for the U.S.?*

Reverse Innovation

After eleven years in Nicaragua, having gone through the war, built
a successful $5 million coffee co-op with 3,000 families, married a
Nicaraguan woman, and fathered a son, Paul had no reason or
intention to ever come back to the United States. Nicaragua was
home. But to go on this journey in Latin America, witness the
impact on people's lives, and then realize that the largest consuming
nation in the world was untapped, unaware of this Fair Trade model
for change, seemed to leave him no choice: "I didn't want to come
back. I *had* to come back and see if I could take this amazing thing
that was going on in Europe and plant the seeds in the U.S."

Paul's mission was clear: how could he help farmers become
part of a different structure that could reassert itself in the global
economy in an empowered way that helps feed the family and
develop the community? To him that was what fair trade was all
about. To achieve it, he determined that the underlying core principles were organization, entrepreneurship, and the marketing of
this value proposition to the consumer. For Paul, it's not just about
technical assistance, training, and boosting quality and yields. Nor
is it just about access to capital. The third leg of the stool is access to
markets, and that means an educated consumer. If you don't have
all three elements, sustainable development will remain elusive.

From Microlending to Market Linkage

Accordingly, Paul is convinced that market linkage is the next big thing to hit the development world and the innovative contribution that Fair Trade USA is bringing to the table. As microfinance reenergized and reordered the development world twenty years ago, building market linkages that connect and grow demand for sustainable products will be the next emergent conventional wisdom. It will have ripple effects for farmers and consumers as well as for the business community. Increasingly, it is also having ripple effects in the activist community, which Paul feels the Fair Trade movement is still a part of.

Conventional wisdom in the business community used to be that profitability and sustainability were at odds with each other. To the extent that a company pursued profitability, it couldn't afford to care too much about sustainability. To the extent that companies pursued sustainability, they had to sacrifice profits. Today, companies are discovering that you can accomplish both at the same time. In fact, some would even argue that sustainability increasingly enables long-term growth, profitability, and brand strength. The Fair Trade movement is helping to create a growing sense that you can break that contradiction and create a better model of capitalism; one that could be categorized as enlightened self-interest. It's a model that is sparking a broader debate and creating a phenomenon that transcends the number of companies that venture into the Fair Trade space. As Harry Smith, a gourmet products importer, recently told Paul:

> Ever since we started to buy Fair Trade products we noticed our customer base increased and people started to ask for these certified products by name. We now buy over $1 million worth of products each month and we hope this will increase as our

consumers realize that they can use their money to make world change with every purchase they make.

As Paul looks back at his earlier years, he reminisces,

I was an anticapitalist in my youth. The twenty-year-old me thought that companies were basically greedy and we needed to pressure and force them to do better. But now, I don't think that confrontational approach works very well in changing corporate behavior. My time in Nicaragua taught me that markets can actually be an incredibly powerful force for lifting farmers out of poverty. I found that by engaging companies and building partnerships with farmers based on common interests, we enabled everyone to win—farmers, companies, and consumers alike.

Paul often advises a reluctant company to start slow and small. If a company is not sure that consumers will pay 5–10 percent more for a fair trade product, it is encouraged to test the idea. The consumer reaction will determine the outcome. It's a less ideological approach—a more pragmatic one based on engagement. It's illustrative of the new breed of activists that Fair Trade is not only a part of but enabling—one that doesn't just rail against the world's injustices but supports powerful, positive alternatives to them. It's a concept that college campuses across the nation are embracing:

So if ever there's an age to be a butt-kicker, it's at age twenty. And twenty-year-olds across the country are embracing fair trade as a powerful, positive alternative. Instead of shutting the university down, they are going to the university dining hall managers and saying "look at this cool fair trade thing, and we'll reward you by supporting what you are doing." It works and it's inspiring activists to rethink their strategies because they see that they are actually moving the needle. They're getting companies to start down this virtuous path, which slowly but surely is having a measureable impact on lives around the world.

The old model of global capitalism puts supply stability at risk; it creates all kinds of reputational challenges because someone, somewhere is going to discover child labor in the supply chain or tons of pollution spewing out of the factory. The emerging logic is that sustainable supply chains are good for business, so sustainability is moving from the realm of corporate social responsibility and philanthropy into the core business model itself. Fair Trade is becoming an integral part of the sustainable supply chain movement because it brings with it strong environmental standards, strong labor standards, and the added value of independent verification and independent auditing that is similar to the organic certification market. You can't just say you are organic and you can't just say you're a Fair Trade item. You need to be certified by a credible, independent third-party organization.

Who You Help by What You Buy

Many companies, whether they support Fair Trade or not, have seen the growth and success of Fair Trade as proof that sustainable supply chains are good for business. They see that consumers have an appetite for sustainable products and in fact are willing to pay a little more for them. This has sparked a number of different initiatives and a lot of competitors. Fair Trade is definitely a powerful example of what Paul argues is a macrotrend toward ethical sourcing and sustainable consumption, and quite possibly a major shift in global capitalism. Corporations are starting to see that it is in their own interest to implement socially responsible labor practices and environmental sustainability. The new face of capitalism is looking more sustainable and responsible. Of course, there are still powerful voices that say Adam Smith was right, and maintain that there's no value in sustainability from a consumer perspective. The trajectory of Fair Trade would argue the opposite: consumers are buying sustainability and they are buying the emotional attribute of feeling that they are on the right side of history, doing no harm and making a difference.

Paul returned to the United States in 1994 thinking his mission was all about farmer empowerment. And Fair Trade became a potent tool to do just that, because it harnessed the participation and the power of the consumer. In turn, that propelled the cycle of buying that encouraged the farmers to grow better products. He soon realized that it's as much about empowering consumers as it is about empowering farmers and workers. His experience shows him that people in America are not indifferent to the suffering of the world nor to climate change and all the other social and environmental challenges of our time. They are concerned, but they don't know how to help. They are also struggling to put food on their own tables, so many don't have time to think about farmers, they don't have time to write letters to the editor, or sometimes even make time to vote. And many don't think their solitary voice makes a difference. But everyone eats and everyone wears clothes, so why not help people everywhere raise their voices by using every dollar they spend as a vote for a better world?

Paul is convinced that everyone becomes part of a virtuous cycle when they turn an act of consumption into an act of grace and good will. When consumers turn something as simple and mundane as a cup of coffee into a way to reach across continents and lend a helping hand to a farming family so they can keep their kids in school, it's incredibly powerful. And the rapidly growing sales of Fair Trade products in the United States—whether coffee, bananas, flowers, or the materials used to make T-shirts—are bearing witness to the fact that consumers want to make a difference and help others though their shopping decisions. Once people visualize the impact of their buying choices, they want to be a part of the solution, and that's the key to the success of Fair Trade.

It's so easy. Choose this coffee instead of that coffee. Choose this banana instead of that banana, and you can be part of this amazing movement for solving the world's problems. In this case every consumer really can be a changemaker, and that indeed is what it will take.

CHAPTER 10

Shit Business Is Serious Business—Nigeria

Social entrepreneur, former security and intelligence officer, and founder of DMT Mobile Toilets, Isaac Durojaiye (also known as Otunba Gadaffi) has established a social enterprise based on a new cultural phenomenon around the availability and use of mobile plastic toilets as public toilets in Africa.

Shit business is serious business. Everyone must go to toilet. Going to the toilet is the only thing you can't delegate to anybody else. No matter how big, no matter how rich you are, you can never ask someone to go to the toilet on your behalf. You've got to do it yourself at least once or twice a day. So going to the toilet becomes very important to everyone. If six or seven billion people go to the toilet at any given moment, then it must be seen as a global phenomenon as well as a serious business opportunity. Your clients will never be limited. The idea that sanitation can be turned around into business—where people can make money out of sanitation and the idea that sanitation when properly managed could improve people's life, people's health, people's well-being while at the same time positively impact the workforce of that nation—makes sanitation and waste management a very good thing to get involved with. Accomplishing all these things together in my work gladdens my heart and makes me feel greatly satisfied.

— ISAAC DUROJAIYE A.K.A. OTUNBA GADAFFI

NIGERIA IS ONE OF SEVERAL COUNTRIES IN AFRICA AND ASIA WHERE the concept of a public toilet is strange to a large percentage of the population. To people living in places where a private toilet, or any type of toilet with a running water source to whisk away waste, is taken for granted, Isaac's statement and his innovation are simplistically beautiful. The entire concept of DMT Mobile Toilets is based on a virtuous business cycle Isaac created to implement a holistic vision of sustainable waste management where none had ever existed. From the culturally sensitive design of the toilets to their construction by local people to the cleanliness of the experience, the strategic placements in areas of need, and the franchising to single-head-of-household women, Isaac has managed to create a societal shift toward the acceptability of the use of public toilets. As he elevates the concept of sanitation to encompass a respectable livelihood, he is lifting an age-old taboo on the topic, the practice, and the behavior.

Two Toilets for Ten Thousand People?

Just how does someone decide to go into the business of toilets in a country where—when pressed—people have used the streets, bushes, walls, and secluded (and not so secluded) spaces as acceptable places of relief for centuries? Isaac never imagined nor intended to be a toilet entrepreneur. At 1.8 meters (6 feet 11 inches) and weighing over 136 kilos (300 pounds) this gentle giant was a security (bodyguard) and intelligence officer whose job was to protect well-known politicians and wealthy Nigerians. While waiting for his clients to be done with their meetings, whenever he needed to relieve himself, Isaac would need to find a secluded outdoor space in the nearby bush. Being such a large man, it was difficult for him to be out of sight! Whether neatly dressed in a suit or in more casual attire, he felt dirty and indecent to be doing his business outdoors in sight of many others. There were rarely, if ever, any toilets around—shops and restaurants did not have the space for even one—and most had no running water for flushing. The words *privacy* and *toilet* were not commonly placed within the same thought process, and those types of facilities were a luxury, not an everyday occurrence.

While developing the security plan for a wedding with about ten thousand guests, Isaac realized that the venue had only two toilets. *Two toilets!* And no one seemed to think this was unusual. Since guests going into the bushes represented a security risk, the only way to improve the situation was to bring in portable toilets. Four weeks later, after scouring the country, no one could come up with any. That was the moment that Isaac recognized a need he could fill. He started to toy with the idea of fabricating them, and came up with eighteen makeshift toilets for the crowd to use. Not long after the wedding, he decided to quit the security job and venture into the toilet business full time.

And it has become a serious business, one that grew from the initial idea around fabrication into a sustainable sanitation and public health program that is spreading across Africa and to toilet-less regions around the globe. An estimated 2.6 billion people, about 40 percent of the world's population, have no access to toilets and defecate anywhere they can. When human waste isn't contained or flushed down a toilet into a regulation sewage system, it can be found everywhere—in streets, open fields, and most dangerously in places that let it filter into the water people drink. As a result, more than 1.5 million children die per year from complications of chronic diarrhea.[1]

In 1999, when Isaac went into the business, Nigeria had fewer than five hundred functional public toilets. As 2011 drew to a close, there were more than five thousand public toilets in the country, mainly thanks to DMT, and the government had contracted for seventeen thousand additional toilets to be placed at schools all over the country. Those twenty-two thousand toilets are operated by thousands of franchisees all over Nigeria—all earning more than they could have dreamed possible, all feeding their families and putting their children through school. And because people don't defecate out in the open anymore, the entire public health system is improving. The public as well as the government has taken notice of the economic as well as the major social benefits for the entire country.

Toilet Marketing 101

The initial idea was somewhat simple and responsive to apparent needs—figure out what type of toilet would be acceptable and manufacture it. But Isaac soon found that toileting had a lot more to do with culture than one might think.

Unfortunately, many people in the world do not understand this important aspect of Isaac's approach. Nigeria's population of about 150 million people has different cultures and multiple religious groups. He wanted to be environmentally sensitive and planned to develop chemically flushed eco toilets. But he soon saw the complexities he faced:

> *If you take an eco-toilet to Nigeria's Muslim community up North, it was not going to be successful, because the cultural and the religious aspects require that when a Muslim goes to the toilet, they clean themselves with water. If you take a dry toilet to such a community, it is not going to work. However in the southern part of Nigeria where water is an extremely valuable resource, squat toilets and their minimum use of water along with a chemically based eco toilet would be a big plus. Another consideration was for women who, as was tradition, wore long and flowing robes. They would be most comfortable if they only minimally had to lift their robes while using a squat style toilet.*

Isaac quickly grasped that toilet and culture went hand in hand, and people needed to have toilets that were suitable for their way of life—otherwise they would not use them. Though each toilet had to share ease of use and maintenance, he needed to design what he calls "the appropriate technology for the appropriate society." With intuitive business acumen and pure marketing savvy, Isaac's ability to create a product that satisfied a serious need meant that it could indeed market itself. The ability to merge need, toilet, and culture with opportunistic placements became one of his greatest market advantages.

The business as well as the social aspects started to come together in Isaac's mind and he was getting excited about the impact that his innovation could have on a number of areas. So instead of merely adding a component that included hiring employees to maintain and clean the toilets, he decided to create a catalytic cycle of social change that overlapped with a more business-oriented sustainable waste management cycle. Both as a social benefit and a business decision he decided to turn his model into a franchise structure, which was based on his mother's struggles as a single parent. The toilets would be leased to single-head-of-household women. (He has now expanded that model to include at-risk youth.) The franchisees would be contractually obligated to keep the toilets spotlessly clean and in exchange they would keep 50 percent of the profits from each of their leases.

The "Pay-As-You-Shit" or coin-operated business model was predicated on a sustained volume of use; for people to use the toilets, they had to have a pleasant experience, which included a clean interior. And at the end of the day, cleanliness would also go a long way toward making Isaac's proposition a bonus for public health. It became obvious to Isaac that the business and social side of the project could merge just as seamlessly as the design and cultural considerations had.

The women franchisees seemed to take more pride in maintaining and cleaning toilets if they knew they were playing an important role in society and in the health of their community. And the community acceptance of their role reinforced their resolve and attitude. Ultimately, of course, profit is definitely important as well, and as one operator said, "I tell you what, shit money doesn't smell at all. Shit gives me a job, it sends my children to school, it buys our food and it gives the entire community a better life. Shit is like gold to me."

Location, Location, Location

It is no doubt difficult for people who have modern toilet facilities to appreciate the lack-of-access issues and the cascading effect they have on a community. Isaac and his team are necessarily always on the lookout for placement opportunities—as both a business proposition and a social decision. For example, he donated a toilet to be placed at a busy ambulance station when he heard that the drivers had missed a call for help while they were defecating in the bush and they were so far away that they could not hear the people shouting for them. DMT Mobile Toilets services that toilet for free, maintains it for free, does everything free of charge. Isaac felt it was his responsibility to society to provide something that would help keep the ambulance personnel at the ready whenever they are needed.

Similarly he has donated more than two hundred toilets to various public schools in Nigeria. This has dramatically reduced the level of absenteeism among girls and students who were sick with dysentery as well as decreased the number of scorpion stings and snake bites among students, who could now stay out of the bushes. Isaac gets immense joy from hearing these impacts and knowing that his product and services have brought such relief to the whole community. Parents are happier as well and the women who operate the toilets have become community heroes.

Owning a Toilet, Controlling Your Life

A serious toilet operator will work about twelve hours a day, six days a week, using one of the days for thorough cleaning and maintenance. On average, an operator can make 1,400 Naira a day ($9) and 26,000 a month ($164). That is a lot of money in Nigeria for a toilet operator to have. This income is for only one toilet (and many operators have multiple leases). And the amount will surely increase as toilet behavior becomes normative. Also, some toilets—if well placed at the beach, for example—are even busier and can serve up to a hundred people a day, bringing in about 56,000 Naira a month ($353). This is more than some Nigerian college graduates have the ability to earn.

And here is yet another delicious ingredient in Isaac's virtuous cycle. The average toilet lease arrangement is for twelve to eighteen months, and after that a serious operator will have paid enough along with the monthly franchise fee to cover a loan on toilet ownership. The toilet becomes theirs. They actually get to own their own asset—knowing well that if they don't maintain and clean it properly, their earnings will diminish. This part of the cycle becomes sustainable and the beneficial impact trickles down to family, friends, and neighbors, adding to the economic stability of the community. A win-win situation for all involved.

Consider Mrs. Adeyinka "Mama Dayo" at Ojodu Berger Bus Terminus in Lagos, one of Isaac's single-mother franchisees, who leases fourteen toilets from him. She has four children and they have all helped her at one time or another to maintain the toilets. From the money she has made, she has put all four of her children in school and sent two of them to the university. When Dayo, her oldest son, was about to graduate, he asked Isaac to help him develop a revolutionary new idea based on the DMT Mobile

141

Toilets model. He wanted to start a business that would keep the streets of Lagos clean. Dayo is now becoming a changemaker who uses and evolves Isaac's vision and applies it to a new business venture that again fulfills another huge social need.

Value Added

And still there are challenges and obstacles. As the toilets become more efficiently fabricated and more widely used, the question of what to do with the waste becomes a pressing one. When Isaac had to pay the government for dumping the waste, he was never too sure of what they did with it. He started to get concerned because he had no idea if the waste was being treated or if it might be ending up in the lagoon polluting the drinking water of another community. So he decided to deal with this uncertainty by setting up a biogas plant so he could recycle the waste and therefore take control of the end product by not having to send it to a government dump site. He is building a plant that converts human waste material to fuel and uses it to generate electricity; the remaining sludge will become an organic fertilizer, which he intends to donate to farmers so they can improve their food production. Isaac's overlapping catalytic cycles of social change are doubling and tripling his impact in a variety of important ways. He maintains, "Any nation that is well fed, any nation that is well protected, any nation with good sanitation, with good public health and with good social amenities will become a great nation."

Sanitation is more important than independence.

—MAHATMA GANDHI

Isaac is convinced that change does not have to come from the top. It has to come from enough individuals so that a positive shift can be felt quickly at the lowest socioeconomic strata: "When you give people dignity you give them a sense of self-accomplishment, a way to carry themselves and a way of being a part of the positive change that is required in the world. When you spread respect you spread it to all people and it spreads rapidly like fire." In fact, this brings Isaac to what he calls the ABCD of toilet:

Toilet must be Architecturally acceptable to the people. That is the A. For the B, there must be a change in people's Behavior and attitude towards using the toilet. And C, the toilet must be Clean. The cleanliness of the toilet is key. And D, the Disposal of the waste in the proper way is very, very important. That is the ABCD of a very good toilet and a waste management system.

Isaac perceives his newest challenge to be the solution mechanism for 2.6 billion people all over the world who do not have access to good sanitation and are suffering from preventable diseases like cholera, dysentery, typhoid fever, and diarrhea. He is starting in his local community, in Lagos, then Nigeria, then West Africa, then Africa, but he recognizes that many people in the world are toilet-less. It is a global phenomenon, and there is a need for a global approach:

What works in Nigeria might as well work in Ghana, then work in Afghanistan, then work in Peru, then work in Brazil. So if the solution is a solution that is workable, is applicable, and adaptable, then it is going to be replicated all over the world as long as the result is to improve humans' life, and to improve humans' dignity.

Isaac's business prototype is wrapped into an employment incentive model that would be lauded in the United States as well as any other region of the world. He is a true example of system

143

change by way of using market forces to create social value. In this case his largest behavioral competitor is cultural inertia (relieving yourself in the streets, bushes, and behind buildings), lack of general sanitation practices, and the mind-set that a toilet is a dirty place. The social part of his business model is based on the prevailing economic and social system in Nigeria and most African countries—a large amount of out-of-work youth, unequal access to sanitation resources (toilets and running water) for a large portion of the population, an absence of opportunities for women, and the lack of a sanitation or public health infrastructure. Isaac is taking cultural obstacles and turning them into social assets by creating value that extends way beyond the provision of a space and a place.

CHAPTER 11

Putting the Public Back in Public Housing—France

Francois Marty is turning the construction, public housing and employment worlds on their head with his integrated approach to supplying the high-quality, ecologically designed housing for the poor using local materials, mixing ancestral and modern construction techniques, and training and employing people previously excluded from the workforce.

FROM A MAN WHO ASPIRED TO BE A TRUCK DRIVER BECAUSE HE thought if he was always on the road his life would seem like one big vacation, comes a multidimensional ecologic, economic, and social program of such vision that it is difficult to know where to start telling the story. Francois Marty has created an ecosystem that is hard to describe. Everything he told me about his past, however far afield it sounded from what he has now created, seemed magically to be just what was needed to lead him directly to what he should be doing—which is exactly what he is doing today. His life story gives credence to the saying "Everything happens for a reason." Each twist and turn of his life has pushed him one step further in the evolution of his ideas. It all started with his desire to help young people whose lives resembled his own youth: poor, not well educated, a little wild, with a cloudy future.

Innovation with Exovation

What began as a consumer-oriented lumber business with a profit-making motive turned into a means to create jobs for a disenfranchised community in Northern France. It is now the largest paper shipping pallet manufacturer in France. Along the way Francois realized two important things that he needed to do to have a successful, sustainable business. He needed to mitigate job retention issues by developing a system that would start at the training end for new hires. And he would also have to employ the principle of *exovation* a term he invented (to signify the opposite of *innovation*), which involves abandoning materials from outside the area and relearning how to use local materials—clay, straw, hemp, and certain types of wood—that were traditionally used to build homes. The term is a combination of the words *exorcize* and *innovation* and it also applies to Francois's facetious wish to exorcize

147

engineers unable to make uncomplicated machines for people who are not complicated.

Francois attributes his ability to accomplish what he has achieved to a simple insight: "I am not here to help the community, I am here to be an entrepreneur with them." His idea is not to have people follow him but to empower them so they can use his ideas and his methodology to go further than he can. He measures himself by an interesting standard: he knows that he has a good idea when he sees people take it and come up with an even bigger one. He is all about letting the people he works with become the changemakers and dare to jump ahead of him. He loves seeing this happen and delights in giving them the support to flourish. This, he says, works to his benefit as well, for whenever it happens, he always learns something new that he then can apply to something else.

Reinventing Development

The immense lumber yard that helps produce Francois's pallets and the materials for the eco-houses he builds is always buzzing with activity. Men and women of all ages are sawing, running machinery, driving the tractors, and generally making the place bustle with energy. As Francois teaches and trains groups of socially rejected people in lumber construction and ecological building production, he makes a special effort to treat women as equal to men, as they rarely have chances to work and succeed in this sector. He normally lets women work the afternoon shift, which is, he observes, when they prefer to work:

> *Women have two different moments in the day. Because when a woman works and her husband is not working (as many immigrant husbands have difficulty finding work), she is even more a slave at home. If the women work in the afternoon until dark, their husbands*

148

are the ones who have to first prepare food in the evening and put the kids to sleep before they can watch football. Otherwise the women work a normal day and then come home and have to take care of the meals and the kids and the house and everything falls on them.

Francois came to his innovative and "exovative" ideas in a roundabout way. He was brought up by parents he describes as "extreme ecologists." In his late teens, the difficult-to-manage Francois went to spend four years in a monastery in the Alps. He attributes everything he learned in those four years—from spelling to reading to history—to his study of the Bible. When he left the monastery, he was ready to realize his dream of becoming a truck driver. But somehow he ended up working and living in a sort of freewheeling hippie community in the south of France, where he met his wife-to-be. His wife's father was a farmworker, and a poor one at that, whose nine children barely had enough to eat. Nonetheless, he made sure that all nine children learned to read and study. He himself spoke four languages, and when he lost his sight later in life, he was able to recite Tolstoy by memory in Russian. Francois's father-in-law became an archetype of sorts for him, demonstrating that even a farmworker could be a genius and manage to bring up nine children who all were educated and positioned to succeed in life.

While Francois was in the south of France, a Catholic priest asked him to come to the north and help work with a community of Iranian refugees. Francois and his wife decided to move to Calais to see how they could best help the immigrants carve out a life for themselves in France.

Mother of Invention

"If we had had the money," Francois recalls, "we never would have gotten the ideas."

Francois started the lumber business as a way of getting intractable youth into meaningful work. At the same time, he knew from his experiences in southern France that lack of affordable and adequate housing was an issue at the root of much immigrant family misery and a large factor limiting the chances for any members of the family to lift themselves out of poverty and into a successful and sustainable way of life. So he decided to combine the consumer-oriented pallet business (the prime source of his incoming funds) with the development of a new type of public housing innovation he calls "Chenelet." Chenelet (a type of strong, hardy oak that grows in the meadows and also the name of the district where the sawmill was begun) is based on creative ecological design principles and new construction processes with the hope of giving youth a more stable and secure place to grow up.

Francois knew that even though it is more expensive to build, eco-housing dramatically lowers the overall cost for the home-owner or renter, who has to be able to afford not only a monthly house payment or rent but also the ever-increasing cost of water, electricity, and heat. It seemed like a perfect marriage of two complementary businesses. One supplies the lumber, the other builds affordable housing to a new standard. The result is aes-thetically pleasing houses, incorporating all the elements clients want, even placing windows so residents can see the neighbors, or using doors that enable the elderly in wheelchairs to see outside. The design for the houses also features wooden floors, superior noise and heat insulation, and clay walls, along with lots of natural light, wood-burning stoves, and rainfall collection mechanisms to minimize utility bills. He then found traditional ecological mate-rials and construction techniques to fulfill these demands. One of Chenelet's prime missions is to shift the perception of the value of such a house, so that its worth is measured over time and not at construction. And now he is working with banks to create new types of loans with longer payouts to give low-income groups access to real estate.

In the process of developing the eco-housing business, Francois never lost sight of his original goal: to help youth with problems find meaningful and satisfying work. He realized that with the expansion of his ecologic vision he could dramatically expand his employment capacity. However, he also realized that his employees would be, for the most part, simple people with simple skills who could not operate complex machinery. So he challenged his engineers to design uncomplicated machines for uncomplicated people. As Francois put it, "I exorcized all the engineers who were developing machines that only highly skilled and educated people could use. And even they had trouble."

Francois was able to redesign almost all the machines used for the cutting and manufacturing of wood for use as lumber. Though most of the wood used for building materials in this region of France has traditionally been imported because the local trees were regarded as offering inferior height and strength, Francois's equipment magic included one machine that could tightly cut, fuse, and glue planks of the local wood together, making them stronger than most imported quality woods. Hence, Francois was able to demonstrate that his principles of exovation coupled with innovation could sustain two industries where none existed before.

All Angles Considered

One by-product of the eco-housing business is its ability to train engineers to think differently. Pierre Gaudin is a classically trained engineer who joined Chenelet in 2009 after working at the largest construction company in the world. He is ecologically oriented and always has been, but in his last job, he says,

They were working to develop earth-building construction. They were not working to build for the people. It's a
totally different perspective. And that's what I love here. We are
not just building with materials from the earth to improve the
technique or the process of doing so, but we are using ecology
as means to improve public housing options and affordability.
It gives my work a new meaning.

Then there was the serendipitous encounter with an influential
benefactor that provided Francois with an opportunity to get his
MBA when he was at the initial stages of building his businesses.
The MBA degree, and what he learned while earning it, helped
Francois to write, advocate for, and see the passage of three laws
that provided incentives and low interest rates for businesses such
as his that had a social purpose attached to them. One of the
laws is aimed at reforming the way the government is buying and
purchasing services, so that "cheaper" is not the criterion that wins
contracts, but ecological soundness is.

The Chenelet brand now covers eight social enterprises, all
with different functions but united in purpose and focus. He
has made the name *Chenelet* synonymous with both quality (the
highest-quality ecologic housing for the poor) and a methodology
that uses local natural materials, mixes ancestral and modern
construction techniques, and trains and employs people previously
excluded from the workforce. With Chenelet's help and tutelage,
impoverished cities and towns all over France are developing their
eco-businesses. For example, Revin, a small depressed town in
northern France, is co-building houses with Chenelet to learn
the techniques to develop its own eco-industry. It recently decided to renovate a large building in town and develop a factory
modeled after Chenelet's sawmill so they can produce their own
building materials. Between the factory and the housing business,
the people of Revin are starting to revitalize the town with new

employment opportunities, training programs, and affordable and sustainable housing.

It's Not Like Running a Chain Store

From practical knowledge Francois knows that you can't fit everything into your own experience. You need to try on someone else's experience to grow and to find a new way, a new system. Though he is a great admirer of the McKinsey business model, he strongly feels that you should fit the McKinsey model to the project—not the other way around. As he expands the Chenelet model throughout France and internationally to French-speaking Morocco, his idea was not to do it himself in other parts of his country and the world but to find other groups, associations, and organizations who are dreaming about the same thing. He encourages them to organize as they choose—as long as they limit their salaries and focus on service to the poor related to social housing. In 2010, seventeen organizations representing a capacity of eight hundred employees formed a French network to develop public eco-housing options. One of Chenelet's social enterprises does the investing and contributes the financing.

Francois and his team are wary of growing too fast and losing the values that should always be a priority when working to improve lives. They know that getting people in the network to work together takes time, as does learning what Chenelet does and adapting it to another environment. It's not like building a chain store. The houses, the materials from the local environment, the financing models, and the laws all need to be modified for each region. Francois likens the network to Linux—it's open-sourced with shared experiences.

Francois's spread strategy, like everything Francois does, is simplistic and humble. He doesn't sell a system, he sells brotherhood and a way to think outside people's existing systems, no matter how different their systems are from his own or each other. Everyone will use different materials and different construction methods, but seeing them doing it gives everyone new ideas:

> *With some partners we have a strong economic link—with others we just want to light their way. We are not trying to build a new product like petrol pumps. We are trying to build a solidarity among people who build for the poor. This will develop the sector and make each organization in it stronger. When you speak with your soul, everyone can understand everything.*

No Tax on Investment

Chenelet is shifting the vision of public housing as being ecological and affordable and Francois is demonstrating its economic viability. He is also creating an entirely new sector of social enterprise while creating employment in ecological construction for those most marginalized. In doing so, he guarantees a strong economic return for social housing operators and social construction enterprises while making a powerful environmental and economic impact in low-income areas.

At the same time Francois is increasing construction capacity in a sector that is experiencing a real shortage of workers. And the biggest shortfall is in construction for ecological buildings. Chenelet takes the triple bottom line, which accounts for people, planet, and profit, and expands it to a quintuple bottom line, which also includes sustainable change and personal fulfillment. As Francois says, "When you invest in human value—there are never any taxes. You come out richer no matter what happens."

Advancing Full Citizenship

Full citizenship means creating equality or supporting human rights for those who don't seem to have a full share of life as many of us know it—due to class, ethnicity, gender, religion, poverty, or physical and mental abilities. This section has much to do with giving people an entry into the economic mainstream—equalizing their chances to advance themselves, their families, and their societies. These chapters deal with struggles to obtain full equity by differently abled people, those who are socially excluded, and those who, by virtue of where they are born and in what society they grow up, may live in misery for most if not all of their lives. Sometimes referred to as the disadvantaged or downtrodden, these are the people who are so limited in their opportunities that they don't even have the freedom to explore a different way of living.

The social entrepreneurs profiled in this section are examples of the many Ashoka Fellows who work to advance full citizenship among all segments of the world's population. Their goals are to co-create a systemic change that nurtures and empowers a part of society previously excluded from being considered capable of changemaking, and who will in turn provide the strength and role modeling needed to ensure the creation of a new reality for those to come.

REFLECTIONS BY GEETA RAO GUPTA

Economic and social inequities are fault lines that threaten to undermine the very foundation of our political, economic, and cultural institutions. When any one member of society is excluded from civic life on the grounds of income, sex, race, caste, or gender, we all bear the consequences. Individuals who are denied the freedom of civic participation cannot contribute to the productivity, innovation, and intellect needed to sustain our households and animate our societies.

Income inequality, experienced most acutely by those who live in poverty, is a barrier to civic participation. Yet advancing citizenship requires more than wealth creation alone. Poverty is multidimensional. The poor are constrained not only by limited economic resources but by the social distance that separates them from the better-off segments of society who control and exercise power. Although important, wealth alone does not guarantee one's acceptance into political, economic, or civic life. Admission into these institutions is mediated by the politics of identity. Whether a society chooses to exclude or include individuals

157

on the grounds of income, sex, race, or religious affiliation directly impacts the household incomes, educational attainment, and health outcomes of the groups affected.

My own work focuses on the inequities experienced by women and children. Economic and social inequities deny women the right to realize their self-potential, to stimulate growth, and to reap the emotional and financial benefits of individual productivity. The consequences reverberate throughout society and across generations. When women are not productive, their children suffer. And when society utilizes only half of its capacity, the fruits of its labor are fewer and less rich. Simply put, economic and social exclusion is a grave injustice with enormous economic costs to women, children, and society as a whole.

Too often, we hear discrimination rationalized as a function of personal attitudes and behavior, largely confined to the private realm and beyond the reach of public authorities. Our efforts to combat violence against women and children have exposed the flaw in this line of argument. Domestic violence is a clear violation of international human rights standards and imposes stiff costs on society. Addressing domestic violence requires policy interventions—concerted action to protect and support victims of violence and punish perpetrators. Policy actions can also play a powerful role in rectifying other injustices suffered by women and other disadvantaged members of society.

There is a strong economic rationale for addressing inequities. In 2010, UNICEF responded to evidence of widening disparities between rich and poor children by questioning the conventional wisdom that it is too costly to address the hardest-to-reach children and communities.

A modelling exercise involving some 180,000 data points from fifteen countries showed that a deliberate focus on the poorest and most marginalized is not just right in principle—it is right in practice.

Each $1 million invested in equity-based approaches would avert up to 60 percent more child deaths than existing approaches to child health and survival. Sharpening our programmatic focus on equity is the quickest and most cost-effective strategy for accelerating progress toward the Millennium Development Goals, especially in low-income, high-mortality countries.

By promoting inclusive public policies and extending health, education, and protection programs to those who need them most, it is possible to bridge inequities and stimulate social inclusion. Doing so is the surest way to create the conditions that will empower the most disadvantaged members of society to exercise full citizenship.

Geeta Rao Gupta is former president of the International Center for Research on Women. She is presently a senior fellow at the Bill & Melinda Gates Foundation and the deputy director of UNICEF.

CHAPTER 12

Financial Freedom for Children — Global

Founder of Childline India, ChildHelpline International, Aflatoun, and Child and Youth Finance International, Jeroo Billimoria has spent the last fifteen years working to eliminate the abuse of children. Starting with the physical abuse of street children then moving upstream to tackle the lack of financial literacy and access to financial opportunities, she helps guarantee the economic future of children around the world.

PLENTY OF CHILDREN STAY AT HOME WITH THEIR FAMILIES, GO to school, and—by most culturally relevant standards—live an ordinary life. Some even help earn money to support their families. They are the lucky ones. They live at home and have some modicum of family life. But many others, not only in India but around the world, have created their own family and a completely new society by living on the streets. This not-so-exclusive street society exists in almost every country. Some countries call them street children, or urchins; others, gangs; and still others, the unwashed and unwanted. We have multiple names for these children, but for the most part, we just don't focus on their circumstances too much in our daily lives.

In Western societies we don't really live with the problem as an everyday occurrence, though we do sometimes see sporadic glimpses of such children as we go about our daily lives. We rarely think about what we are not seeing. And if we do see it, we become apathetically farsighted. If we live in a place where it is an everyday occurrence, then ironically, almost the exact same thing occurs: we stop seeing it and don't bother to focus our attention on something that happens as a matter of course. We become apathetically nearsighted. Either way, the problem of children and teens living hand-to-mouth on the streets, earning whatever money they can by mostly illegal and illicit means, is not something that makes us comfortable to think about.

Street Smarts

Enter Jeroo Billimoria, an Indian social worker who, in an attempt to understand the life of some of "her street children" clients, actually went to live with them so she could best understand how to help them. She was quite proud of what she was learning on her nocturnal adventures until one night one of the street kids said,

"I live on the streets. You can stay with us, and you think you know us, but you know you have a home to go to when you leave. It's not the same. You social workers go home at night and we have no one here to call for help. It's not the same at all." That remark, combined with what she did see on the streets, did a lot to frame her thinking.

In 1996, Jeroo started Childline India, which in her words was not a prevention program to keep kids off the streets but a way to help them because they were already on the streets and being badly abused. It was a way to be there for them when they were harassed, accosted, or in trouble. It was a way to assist them during the nights (and later, during the day) when they had no place to go and no one to turn to. She built the program out of the most pressing needs that the street children told her they had because she knew that the people most able to understand the street community were the children who lived there.

Childline India offered a free call number for street kids to get help from any public phone. Over time, Jeroo realized that as families broke down, the most entrepreneurial of the kids would take to the streets. This hypothesis got support when, as a result of answering calls through the help hotline, Jeroo noticed that to successfully survive on the street the children had to be brave, smart, persistent, innovative, and creative. They took risks. They had the attributes of business entrepreneurs. But they were totally unsophisticated about money and often exploited financially by older children and adults as soon as they had any money. They were caught in a vortex of poverty that sucked them into a life of prostitution, drug use, and serial illegal activities and created a type of nonexistence that allowed their lives to be unseen, unheard, and unaccounted for.

These observations stayed with Jeroo.

Breaking the Cycle

Childline India became the first of its kind, a twenty-four-hour emergency toll-free telephone service with follow-up support to alleviate the distress of children without other resources. Run by trained street children, it took a holistic approach and partnered with an extensive network of child-service organizations, police officers, and social workers through a franchise model.[1]

News of the India program spread round the world, and by the time Jeroo turned around to take a breath, she had requests for replicating the program coming in from cities and countries worldwide. Understanding that true systems change comes through global efforts, in 2003 she founded ChildHelpline International (CHI). It wasn't long before the program spread to 133 countries and counting. CHI created a network of helpline services and today has answered over 140 million calls. Impressively, given the power of replication and spread, Jeroo and her CHI team were able to inspire a global policy movement and a huge policy change; in 2008, the United Nations International Telecommunications Union adopted a Supplement recommending one number for all toll-free children's helplines in all countries.

But Jeroo was not satisfied, because the program, though wildly successful from anyone's assessment, was not keeping children off the streets in the first place. She wondered what could be done to remove the abuse, what could alleviate the poverty, what could keep children in school, and how she could prevent the vicious cycle of street life from perpetuating itself. She dared ask herself the really tough question: what will ultimately change these children's lives?

It also started from my personal experiences, from the experiences I had when I was young. When my father was very sick, I had to take

163

on the family finances and surprisingly found that I could manage it quite effectively. I was very young, about fifteen, and I could do it because my father had been guiding me every inch of the way.

Saving Children by Teaching Them to Save

Now Jeroo began thinking about herself and how she was empowered by her father to be able to help her family in crisis. She sensed that people don't understand the capacity children have to comprehend money matters, to believe in themselves, and therefore be able to change their lives. And all these thoughts coupled with another simple observation became the genesis for her new program: Aflatoun. Because children normally don't reach the streets before age eight, nine, or ten, they have already had one or more years of primary school. That means that Jeroo just needed to find a way to keep them in school and out of the streets. She decided to tackle the growing numbers of street children at the roots by teaching children enough financial literacy to keep them off the streets in the first place. She developed a school-based program that would rechannel children's entrepreneurial craftiness and their interest in making and having money by providing them with a monumental way to see life through a future lens and not merely a daily one. While CHI would continue to help kids on the streets, her new program, Aflatoun, would start with the kids in school, who were not yet living the street life.

The program is based on two premises: the professional one, which came from Jeroo's roots as a social worker and her drive to prevent any child from having to resort to a life on the streets, and a deeply private reason—Jeroo's firm belief that empowering children socially and economically allows them to become agents of change in their own lives, break the cycle of poverty, and contribute to a more equitable world. For her, the model is based on one word—*trust*: trust for others, and trust in yourself.

Jeroo started Aflatoun to prevent children from being shut out of their economic future by teaching them financial skills at an early age. Her upstream project would help keep them from living on the streets in the first place by teaching them to understand how to use their skills to both earn and save money.

Building a Future

Indeed, the target group for Aflatoun in many countries is poor children. These children will not have much money to save, but experience has shown that many children, even in poor countries, do get small sums of money—from their parents as pocket money, on special occasions from friends and relatives, as scholarships and prizes, or from after-school jobs.

The model presupposes that every human being is an agent of change and all have the capacity of being better than they ever imagined themselves to be. It is based on providing the tools to bring out the enhanced changemaking capacity of each child.

After one year in an Aflatoun program, a child from Burkino Faso had enough savings to buy a second-hand cycle. He began to rent it out, and now he has five cycles and is putting his brother into school along with others in the family. Stories like this abound. Children taking part in an Aflatoun program get their parents, siblings, and the community involved. Mothers who know that their children are learning to save quietly start to give some household money to them to put away. They let them use the money to start micro-enterprises supervised by Aflatoun. Children of one mother used their savings to buy materials to make and sell beaded items.

These microbusinesses, no matter how small, give the children the luxury of using the word "someday" and envisioning a future life. And envisioning a future out of none at all turns nightmares into beautifully sweet and secure dreams. Aflatoun is less concerned with the amounts saved than with instilling the habit of regular saving. Saving, planning, and budgeting have outcomes beyond immediate financial rewards. Of most importance is the future-oriented mind-set the children develop, an orientation that helps lead them away from financial vulnerability and teaches them how best to avoid becoming trapped in debt and poverty.

Leveraging her vast experience in pioneering social enterprises, Jeroo chose the most difficult (poorest) countries first and piloted her venture. After a staggering success in eleven nations, Aflatoun's goal was set to reach more than a million children by 2010. It exceeded that goal by four hundred thousand, spreading its vision and mission by franchising the curriculum and materials among a variety of local partner organizations in more than seventy-five countries.

When the Junior Achievement program of Namibia launched Aflatoun Namibia, the CEO of FNB Namibia Holdings said, "The Aflatoun programme not only teaches but encourages a savings culture in a structured way. A very important sentiment, if you consider that less than 3 percent of Namibians save regularly. We seem to be a nation of spenders, and as such are stuck in a cycle of generational poverty. Aflatoun aims to empower children to make a change and break the cycle of poverty by equipping them with the constructive tools of financial independence."[2] The announcement went on to note that the organization hoped an estimated 100,000 to 150,000 children would be exposed to the FNB program in the four-year period.

Building a System, One Piece at a Time

Aflatoun has reached one of its targets of seeing financial education for children and young people as a topic on the agenda for educators and policymakers in many areas of the world. But again, Jeroo has asked herself more hard questions: How are young people going to achieve financial independence if they don't have access to mainstream finance? How can we change the public policy agenda by creating a structural solution to breaking poverty and increasing empathy?

Since Aflatoun was equipping children with a good financial education, the students would be on the path to making wise financial choices. However, if they wanted to set up their own savings program—or start a small business—they had nowhere to turn for help until, at best, they turned eighteen. To complete the system she started with Childline, Jeroo decided to build yet another interlocking component. In July 2011 Child and Youth Finance International (Childfinance.org) was created with three advocacy goals in mind: to ensure that a hundred million children and youth have access to appropriate and low-cost financial products by 2015; to ensure that a hundred million children and youth have access to Child and Youth financial education by 2015; and to ensure that a hundred countries have in place an action plan supported by Child and Youth Finance International. To alter the age-old perceptions of children's needs and abilities in the realm of finance, Jeroo is planning to coordinate alliances with banks, financial regulatory agencies, national NGOs, and governments. All organizations involved will be invited to become part of the changemaking community. It's a huge effort—and given her track record for large-scale global successes, I have no doubt that 2015 is going to be a big year for children everywhere.

I asked what kept Jeroo going and if and when she saw an end to her mission. Her humble answer was what one would expect from someone who has influenced millions of lives and is solely focused on changing millions more:

I must be doing something right. I don't think about it. Most times—99.999 percent of the time—I don't think about it. Most, I think about what I have to do next. That's the status that I hold myself to.

CHAPTER 13

Overcoming the Barriers Between Us and Them—Germany

Andreas Heinecke, founder and CEO of Dialogue Social Enterprise, has worked for more than twenty years to overcome barriers between "us" and "them" and to redefine *disability* as *ability*, and *otherness* as *likeness*.

WAR, PLASTIC SOLDIERS, AND TANKS WERE HIS CHILDHOOD PASSIONS, and when Andreas was thirteen years old he spent many hours engaging his replicas in battles around the floor. He was quite proud of being German and tried to learn everything he could about World War II. One day while watching a TV documentary about the bombing of Warsaw, he saw a sequence showing Jewish people being transported on the trains to concentration camps. He was so convinced that the Jews were the reason that Germany lost the war that when he turned to tell this to his mother, he was surprised to see her quietly crying. It was then that she told him that parts of his family were Jewish and killed during the war. It was almost too much for him to comprehend, and he finally realized why he had never met any of his mother's relatives.

The next day, Andreas painted all his plastic tanks white with red crosses and instead of playing imaginary battles, he now started to play rescue and began to subconsciously internalize preventing death instead of causing it. He started what became a lifelong process of trying to understand how people can decide which people are more valuable than others. He searched for the reasons that people turn against their friends, their neighbors, and their families, and the factors that make it possible for them to do so. It became a primary preoccupation for Andreas: to find out what turned people from good to evil and how it could happen that millions of innocent people were killed during that war. This interest paved Andreas's way and determined the course of his future.

The Encounter

Only a few years later, while working at a radio station, he was asked to visit a journalist who had recently been blinded in an accident. Andreas was supposed to figure out what sort of job the man could do now that he was without sight. Andreas thought it was all a waste of his time—and that there was nothing they could offer a blind man because he wouldn't be able to do a thing at a radio station.

And I came to his apartment and rang the bell and I felt a little bit awkward. The guy opened the door, he was tall, looked like a rock-and-roller with long hair and a leather jacket. Amazingly he didn't look blind and he actually seemed happy. So I asked if he was Matthias, the person I was looking for, because I could not believe that this man standing in front of me was blind. I followed him in and down the staircase and as he descended the stairs, I told him to be careful. He said don't worry, the blind can walk. Sitting down in his room, he took out a cigarette and I watched him light the end of it. And then he poured coffee while he was walking around and talking to me. He could, of course, do everything rather normally.

I was so surprised that when I left after this interview I was really ashamed and shocked about myself. I was really embarrassed that I, with my education and my family history, could so quickly put him mentally in the distance and not understand that his life is valuable. It felt like I had taken a first step to seeing him as an "other" and that would make it easier to exclude him. And that made me think about how the Nazis made their trial gas chamber experiments with disabled people.

Immediately after this encounter, Andreas went back to learn more about "the differently abled." He learned that 610 million people are disabled worldwide, out of whom 400 million live in the developing world, and 38 million in Europe. Now, not surprisingly to Andreas, the research showed that while they are all labeled *disabled*, only approximately 5 percent of them regard themselves as such. So it seemed that it was the outside world that made the differently abled into the disabled—and not the people who were missing some abilities themselves. The "normal" people were disempowering "the others." He became committed to the cause of diversity acceptance.

Finding True North

Andreas became a documentarian and journalist, and as he observed Matthias's growing success at the radio station in a more analytical way, it occurred to him that he was the one who was more in the dark than Matthias. Andreas had always intended to continue his career at the radio station, but suddenly that sort of life didn't seem to interest him. All of a sudden his life seemed fragmented and unfilled. And then he found his true north, the life direction he knew was right for him.

One day, purely by chance, he discovered himself in a very low lit, almost dark room in the radio station with Matthias. Andreas couldn't see a thing and he realized how helpless he felt and how he depended on Matthias to find their way. He realized how much this experience affected him, similar to his first encounter with blindness. He was again convinced how competent differently abled people can be—even though we don't see them in that way or recognize them as such. He started to think about ways he could shift perceptions by bringing the blind and the sighted together, determining that the only way people would understand the lesson he learned was by exactly the same route—encounter. But to do this he would have to create a situation where there would be total role reversal and positive results, much like he experienced. He had to reverse circumstances to make people understand their own vulnerability, their own limits. He was certain that this knowledge would help them to open up, to perceive things differently. Andreas strongly believed that if he could show the capabilities of blind people to sighted people who had never interacted with a blind person before, they too would be convinced of their abilities. This would be how he could help engender respect for the blind and bring the abled and differently abled together, for mutual learning encounters.

The 360-Degree Shift

Andreas started to experiment with "dark" experiences. He was having fun finding situations that would be safe but adventurous enough to create mind shift. As he tells it,

> *It was 1988 when we first tried a group experience in the dark. And I tried to watch the reaction of my girlfriend in the room. It was a very intimate experience. You are in the dark and you are having a physical encounter but barely seeing anything. And then I saw my girlfriend beside me looking for a kiss. But she moved back before I could respond and there was another lady standing there. I kissed the wrong girl. It was so funny. Funny and totally surprising. It was then that I knew this idea had power.*

Calling his program "Dialogue in the Dark," he established a laboratory for overcoming barriers between "us" and "them"—a platform for immersing people in worlds very different from their own in order to break down prejudices and to communicate and understand barriers that exist across different cultures. It was predicated on action, not words. Sighted people had the chance to experience total darkness in which blind people taught them to see. It was never Andreas's primary intent to turn the experience into one that created jobs for blind people, or one empowering them to go out and get jobs. More important, it was about how to close a mental gap, how to force people on both sides of the dialogue to think differently about each other. Eventually a major focus became the redefinition of *disability* as *ability* and *otherness* as *likeness* through shared experiences.

The idea is simple: In complete darkness, blind individuals lead small groups of people through a series of ordinary situations that are suddenly experienced extraordinarily, without eyesight. As one reporter described the process:

> Visitors are led by blind guides in small groups through totally
> darkened rooms where sounds, wind, temperatures and textures
> convey the characteristics of daily environments such as a park, a
> city or a bar. In the dark, daily routines turn into new experiences.
> The effect is a role-reversal: sighted people are torn out of
> their familiar environments, losing the sense they rely on most: their
> sight. Blind people guide them; provide them with security and a
> sense of orientation, transmitting a world without pictures. The
> blind and partially sighted guides open the visitors' eyes in the dark
> to show them that their world is not poorer—just different.[1]

Rethinking "Others"

Dialogue in the Dark has now transformed into Dialogue Social Enterprise (DSE), a corporation that, by franchising exhibition and exhibit opportunities, has enabled the concept's impact to broaden and result in unparalleled spread and scale. DSE is the laboratory for mind shifting that now encompasses Dialogue in Silence, conceptually similar to Dialogue in the Dark except the focus is on deaf people, and most recently, Dialogue of Generations, which is "an exhibition that will encourage intergenerational dialogue in order to change the public's attitude towards aging. The exhibit will focus on the current demographic age shift that the entire world is experiencing. It will give the elderly a platform where they can share their thoughts, sorrow, dreams and needs."[2]

Complementing the exhibitions are a host of other activities, from educational activities for pupils, teachers, and the general public to business workshops worldwide for large to small companies and institutions. In 2009, Allianz Global Investors (Allianz GI, a global investment and insurance firm) saw the potential for using Dialogue in the Dark workshops for leadership development training. It set up a Dialogue experience as a human resource training center at its headquarters in Munich and implemented workshops for different sets of managers around the world. Gerhard Hastreiter, SVP at Allianz, has been through four Dialogue in the Dark training sessions, three of which he organized for the three hundred employees who report to him. Each time he's come away with something different: "You have to change your perceptions the minute you step into that darkened environment. This in turn causes you to alter your behavior; to slow down; to reflect a little longer; to listen more attentively and to communicate more clearly. You definitely see behavior and team dynamics change as you go through the experience." Allianz GI is using Dialogue as its internal methodology for building trust and leadership. It is a corporation that is changing the face of human resource development in its sector and will no doubt become a model institution for creating a working understanding of diversity. As of 2010, DSE has conducted more than five hundred business workshops for a variety of corporations in various sectors around the globe.

Occasionally, special events are developed to amplify interaction, like the gastronomic experience called a Taste of Darkness where blind waiters serve sighted participants a surprise four-course dinner in complete darkness. DSE now runs wine-tasting parties and concerts in the dark as well. Mind shift indeed!

Understand Diversity and You Understand Humanity

Since 1988 more than 7 million visitors in thirty-five countries have participated in 160 exhibits and events. More than seven thousand jobs for blind and deaf people who are involved in all facets of

DSE has been created. The impact and reaction of exposing people to these types of experiences and encounters has been monumental. Participants are commonly quoted as discovering their own values and humanity while going through the experience or having their worldview completely challenged and changed. INSEAD, one of the leading business schools in the world, introduces Dialogue in the Dark workshops as part of the curriculum in France and Singapore. Along with teaching diversity, INSEAD Professor of Leadership Hal Gregersen maintains, "Dialogue is a powerful medium for provoking powerful change and fostering innovation skills." It now delivers the Dialogue workshop to social entrepreneurs who enroll in its annual social entrepreneurship leadership development programs. DSE had previously developed a "Redesigning Business Leadership" plan and working with business school students through INSEAD was a giant step in this direction.

Not only are DSE's programs throwing a wrench into traditional thinking about blindness and deafness, they are challenging all sorts of thinking and actions around differences among leaders, managers, socioeconomic classes, people of all sizes, shapes, and colors. Dialogue is effecting change in business settings and university classes alike. But at the end of the day it also changes the differently abled themselves, who are for the first time "seeing and hearing themselves in a new light." Tail Elimelech, a Dialogue in Silence human resource manager at the Israeli Children's Museum in Holon, says it best:

> I am a person with many identities. A deaf person, a daughter
> of deaf parents, a mother, a woman, a wife. Everything is mixed
> together. Deafness is strongly expressed in all of these identities.
> For the first time I can put my deafness in a secondary place
> and allow other things to be expressed. My world isn't sliced in
> two when I arrive at work. My world is one. I have the power

to change things, even slightly. Every person who leaves viewing things in our world a bit differently is a success for me—it's so strong, so productive.... I am there, opposite them, opening a window to my world, welcoming them into my world with joy, illuminating their eyes.

Andreas is helping create a world of change by breaking through prejudices, where everyone from business leaders to students to differently abled people can find their place in DSE's catalytic cycle of change that affects us all along with our notions of "others."

CHAPTER 14

Autistic Abilities— Denmark

Thorkil Sonne is founder and board member of Specialisterne, which employs people with autism and enables them to use their computer skills to provide valuable services for the business community.

I don't consider them autistic—they are more like specialists. They have very special qualities that make them focused, detail-oriented, and persistent. Wouldn't we be rewarding these qualities in a person who wasn't labeled as autistic? Why don't we just understand people for what they can do rather than label those who are not like us?

—THORKIL SONNE

THORKIL SONNE WAS DEVASTATED WHEN HIS SON LARS WAS diagnosed with autism at age three. Thorkil was, by his description, a traditional family guy having a traditional life who in his spare time did quite a bit of local volunteer work. Life was good and he was cruising along in fifth gear—until the day his youngest son was diagnosed. It was a life-changing experience for him and his wife. Thorkil suddenly realized that Lars would not have the same chances in life as his older siblings. He pictured Lars as an adult and asked himself, "What will make Lars happy when he gets older; when my wife and I are too old to care for him and carry on his fight? What would it take for him to have a good life?"

It's Not Quite Like the Movies

Thorkil knew nothing about autism except for what he had seen in the movie *Rainman* with Dustin Hoffman and Tom Cruise. He surmised that Hollywood had trumped reality; most everyone who has seen that movie thinks that most people with autism have a skill-set and personality similar to the lead character. In the real world very few people have such extraordinary skills, and certainly less than 1 percent of all people with autism have them. As Thorkil immersed himself in learning about the disorder, he and his wife noticed that in all the books they were reading the prevailing view was that Lars would never get a job and would always have a problematic life. There were no books that told the Sonnes if or how Lars could fit in, only how he would not.

The autism spectrum varies from the severest conditions, where those with the disorder cannot live independently, to the mildest form (called Asperger syndrome, or Asperger's), which was not defined as a disorder until 1994 and can seem little more than extreme social awkwardness. Autism leads to difficulties in relationships, communication, understanding of social subtleties (such as irony and sarcasm), tics and repetitive motions, and a need for comfort and safety in the form of routines and rules and mellow, tranquil environments. Autism is estimated to affect about 1 percent of the population, and attention deficit hyperactivity disorder (or ADHD) may affect another 3–4 percent. Imagine these numbers and the people they represent on a world scale and you can quickly grasp the scope of the challenge worldwide for individuals, families, and society.

Serendipity

As Thorkil and his wife tried to deal with their son's situation, Thorkil realized that Lars's diagnosis had not changed who he was—he was still loving, adorable, and caring, but without friends. The diagnosis meant nothing to him, but to his parents it was a different matter. They noticed that the strain of dealing with Lars's future was filling up more and more time, so they decided that Thorkil would quit his job as a technical director of an IT technology firm to learn as much as he could about how best to help his son not only survive but—if possible—thrive.

Thorkil got involved in the autism society and soon became president of a local branch, a post he held for three years. He absorbed everything he could about the Danish welfare system and supportive nonprofit organizations and also learned from any programs, presentations, or people who could provide answers or inspiration. He found that though there were many welfare support tools for use in Denmark, they were all constructed on the basis of visible disabilities—not invisible ones. He quickly realized that welfare employees were rewarded for not taking risks; the only way they could do their jobs well was to do the same things they have done forever, over and over again. Innovation could never be encouraged in the system if things were to go on as they were. It seemed that no changes would come from the authorities or the traditional labor market because they were both locked into conventional thinking. They would never see Lars as having capacities instead of deficits.

All of Thorkil's research and his work with the autism society influenced his personal framework as well and the way he now related to differently abled children, adults, and their parents. He learned a lot about respecting people and life. Before, if he was at the grocery store and there was a woman with a child who was behaving rather badly, he would internally blame her for not raising the child well or for not being effective at making the child be quiet. Now he considers how brave the mother is and really empathizes with her difficulties and embarrassment. He feels like he wants to go give her a hug, whereas before, his sentiment was anything but.

Going from Fifth Gear to First

Before becoming conscious about autism, Thorkil worked at a telecommunication company that was highly involved with computer systems. As he read about autism, he realized that some of the very talented people he had seen working on computers had exhibited some autistic-like characteristics themselves. They were

183

extremely motivated, particularly attentive to detail, with keen memories and high levels of concentration. They wouldn't stop until they had checked out every detail and were sure everything worked exactly the way it should. They didn't seem to be particularly skilled socially and kept pretty much to themselves. In the right situation with the appropriate job, they seemed to excel. So Thorkil asked himself, "Why couldn't someone labeled as autistic, who had the exact same skill sets, excel under those same conditions?"

To test out his hypothesis, Thorkil set up a market-based company that would fill the niche for consultants who could test new computer software. There seemed to be a large customer base and out of this would come lots of options for people like Lars to excel in the labor market. Specialisterne (The Specialists) was created in 2004. In 2008 he founded the nonprofit Specialist People Foundation with the goal of enabling employment for a million autistic adults throughout the world.

Thorkil is crystal clear about his mission. In simple terms it is an employment agency that contracts with businesses to supply specialized computer consultants who are assessed on their technical rather than social skills. As Thorkil told the *Harvard Business Review*, "This is not cheap labor, and it's not occupational therapy. Our consultants simply do a better job."[1]

A Good Idea That Fills a Need Markets Itself

The reason for this superior performance seems to be that Specialisterne is a mixture of idealism and business, established on a concept so strong that Thorkil says the company was able to fend for itself on market terms right from the beginning:

*No one has ever done it before—so we couldn't read how to do it.
On the other hand that has also meant that we at no time have been*

bound by how things are usually done—we have had free rein to think outside the box.

Most autism therapies focus on molding a person to fit into social situations. Few make reverse adaptations: changing circumstances and perceptions in society at large and in the working world to suit the needs of people with autism that allow them more and better opportunities for integration in the wider world. Thorkil assesses and trains not only his consultants (who are hired on a fixed contract basis) but also the potential employer to make sure that the workplace environment is responsive to the needs of his consultants.

Since the majority of Specialisterne consultants work on site at the client's facilities, creating a comfortable working environment is conducive to productivity and improved behavioral function. In a relaxed setting, things viewed as autistic traits become minimized and just need a bit more understanding. Though Thorkil is quick to add that "people with autism did not invent open space offices," constructing a culture that caters to the requirements of autistic workers is not tremendously different from best practices in any office environment. It incorporates structured working methods, clear instructions, limited stress situations, and working hours adjusted to individual capacities. On Specialisterne's end, during and after the initial five months of intensive employee training, consultants receive ongoing personal support, personalized training, and skill development programs to help ensure a comfortable transition into each new consultation project. The training develops and builds not only market-related abilities but those relevant to daily life as well.

Many of the Specialists express almost identical sentiments to Danish consultant Steffen Møller Pedersen's: "I have a good life now! Through Specialisterne, I have acquired good professional skills, which I really appreciate, and they have also helped to improve my social skills!"

From the client's side, when a company begins to work with Specialisterne, a point of contact is appointed who is empathetic to the skills and limitations of autistic people and trained by Specialisterne in the most effective practices for working with them. Other company employees are given a short introduction to autism, and things to keep in mind when working with autistic people. Several client companies have reported, perhaps not surprisingly, that their employees who are in frequent contact with the autistic software testers have begun to speak more clearly and directly with one another as a result of working with people who require a very explicit style of communication.

At the same time, the client very frequently begins to experience improvements in communications and increased understanding among its other employees as a result of working with Specialisterne's specialists. Says Henrik Nesager, Software Platform Management Service, IBM:

> Working with two interns from Specialisterne, I learned that accommodating their need for well-defined instructions and ensuring optimal work conditions from the start increases their productivity and the quality of the end-result considerably. Teaming up with them was an eye-opening experience and I now use this knowledge with great success when working in other teams. This has also led to an increased satisfaction amongst team members.

From Handicap to Competitive Advantage

Thorkil Sonne is transforming the way society perceives autism—from viewing it as a handicap to recognizing that it can create a competitive advantage. Thorkil's goal is to take people from an unwanted to a wanted place. He calls the journey "The Dandelion Model":

> *Many people consider a dandelion a weed. But I see a weed as nothing but a plant in an unwanted place. If you take the plant from an unwanted place to a wanted place—you turn the weed into an herb. That's the situation for dandelions—and that's the situation for many "specialist" people who do not fit into the mainstream of our society. Place them somewhere where they fit in and they turn into beautiful beings.*

As Specialisterne grows, so do the multiple requests to replicate the model in other cities around the world. Thorkil has been contacted by people in sixty countries, and from twenty-nine states in the United States alone. He was starting to find it impossible to run Specialisterne and spread the model at the same time. After all, how was he to reach his goal of a million global employment placements for "special people" if he could not first attract and then convince others that his system was indeed replicable, functional, successful, and worthy of adoption?

Thorkil's trade-off was whether to continue to grow his own social enterprise or reach his million-placement goal: "I have learned that if you want to scale, you have to let go, you have to inspire and not keep on designing." He decided to grow the model by creating an NGO and grow Specialisterne's financial sustainability by selling its knowledge. To do that, he created the Specialist People Foundation, where other changemakers could learn the management model and earn a Specialisterne license. What he is ultimately conceptualizing is creating an open-source knowledge community that brings everyone into a global network of collaboration that could trigger millions of ideas based on his philosophy. The outcome could be additional adaptations much better suited to local communities than Thorkil and his team could come up with on their own.

Thorkil is not at all interested in building big organizations. He just wants to find local social enterprises or social entrepreneurs who are not simply interested in using the knowledge base but committed to removing the divide between autistic people and society. This can happen if each licensed organization works to inspire others to adopt, adapt, replicate, and spread the model. He knows that in all companies and in all government agencies there will be employees who are also parents—parents of children with all forms of autism, ADHD, and other learning disabilities. Once they are made aware of this life-changing program, he intuits that their inspiration and energy will become a mobilizing force; they will be an army of catalysts embedded in each of their organizations that will make sure that this program succeeds and that all the differently abled specialists have a working environment suited to their own needs.

A Model Turns into a Movement

Thorkil can clearly see the path of mobilization: from Specialisterne to the licensing of social enterprises to support from employed parents of autistic adults (championing the model to their companies and offices), to mobilization of a global movement. He already knows close to twenty organizations that have been inspired by Specialisterne, and with steadfast faith, he envisions hundreds more spreading across both developed and developing countries.

When the need for special help arises, parents tend to get extremely protective toward their kids. As the kids grow older, the parents realize that they will have to let go—and at the same time they are afraid of the possible consequences. It is a cruel choice. By helping the adult children get employment and realize their potential, Thorkil hopes he can help the parents let go with a good conscience. Without this stepping-stone, children with autism will end up living with their parents until their parents can no longer take care of them—and then what?

Lars is only fourteen now, but if he can look forward to the prospect of a job where he would be appreciated and respected for his particular personality, Thorkil knows that he and his wife will be able to retire with diminished concerns.

As our autistic employees go through the training process and then become employed, I see how they grow in self-esteem. They are like computers that need rebooting. It's the most motivating part of my work and a magical moment for me, especially as the father of a boy with autism.

CHAPTER 15

Crazy Becomes Normal—Argentina

Alfredo Olivera created and founded *Radio La Colifata*, the first radio program to use mental patients as broadcasters. The program, originating in Buenos Aires, has an estimated 12 million listeners. Countless more worldwide have heard *La Colifata*'s message through the music, TV programs, and films it has inspired.

WHILE STUDYING FOR HIS DEGREE IN PSYCHOLOGY, ALFREDO Olivera worked Saturdays as a volunteer for Hospital Borda, a 148-year-old institution near Buenos Aires. El Borda is the largest of Argentina's oversaturated and poorly resourced hospitals, and its property includes an outdoor garden where Alfredo's arts and crafts program met. It occurred to him that the beauty of this weekly program was that it opened the doors to volunteers who came from the community and created meeting opportunities inside the psychiatric hospital—but it wasn't working as planned. The patients were mainly impoverished people who had been committed by relatives. Many had been institutionalized for more than ten years. They didn't know how to relate to the outside world coming in. So in actuality it began and ended each Saturday without having any impact on the patients. When all the volunteers packed up and left, the patients remained isolated and socially abandoned. They lived in their own private world within the walls and confines of El Borda. When they were pronounced well enough to leave the hospital, they were lost—emotionally, intellectually, and psychologically—and totally unprepared for life outside.

Demolishing Walls

Alfredo became intrigued by the thought of developing a more meaningful connection with the patients while he was at the hospital, so when friends at a small community radio station asked to interview him on conditions there, he saw his opportunity. Instead of doing a regular radio interview, he decided to interact with the patients by recording their views and playing them on air instead. The idea came to him as he recalled his prior experience in having run a literacy program in a poor community with no supplies, resources, or officially designated space. That experience taught him that a program could grow in a distinctive manner if the students became the constructors of their own school, because such a program could be assembled with the community and operated in just about any physical space. He decided to try to help the patients construct their own radio interview and then assess if it had any impact on their psychological well-being. After all, he was still a student and anxious to learn how best to relate to people in hopes of being an effective psychologist.

The patients seemed to enjoy the interview, and the first tapes aired on the community radio station as planned. They were such a hit with the listeners that Buenos Aires network radio shows very quickly picked them up. Given that success, plus his knowledge of journalism from his journalist father along with his childhood fantasy of being a radio announcer, Alfredo conceived of a radio-type program to help socialize the patients in this overcrowded mental hospital. At the time Alfredo began his project in the early 1990s, the Internet was in a fledgling stage. CompuServe had just begun the first e-mail service one year prior. The world wasn't wired, computers were not part of daily life, and information resources were definitely not available at a click of a mouse. There was no such thing as a reality TV show and no other program anywhere in the world like the one Alfredo envisioned. So Alfredo devised a simple way of using short taped segments that he would send to local radio stations. It was to be the first radio show recorded at a mental institution and the first ever using patients as the broadcasters.

Originally (and to this day), the idea in itself was not about making a radio show; it was about developing an entire process of reconnecting the patients to the community and in doing so create a greater awareness in the community that not all mental patients were dangerous and of little or no value to society. The show's two primary purposes were to provide a way of getting patients to talk about their issues, their pains, and their fantasies, and to re-introduce them to the world outside El Borda. At the same time it aimed to destigmatize mental problems as well as decrease exclusion of mental patients as a societal issue.

Describing the first meeting where a group of patients came together around a table in the garden of the psychiatric hospital to talk about distinctive things in life, Alfredo says:

These conversations were particularly interesting because the things they talked about didn't have to do with a conception based on passing or killing time, or how to make life better at the hospital. Rather they decided to see if they could create a situation that resulted in a gathering of patients who talked about very interesting things. Therefore, the first few themes that they talked about were complex and profound. They decided that the first one should be about the role of women in society.

Psychological Waste Recycled

Because they had no broadcasting equipment, Alfredo would record these conversations on tape and edit them into short audio clips, which radio stations in Buenos Aires would then broadcast to the outskirts of the city. Within weeks, the radio stations started to get calls and comments from listeners about the audio clips. Alfredo would tape the full radio programs, including the comments from the radio station's audience and then play the entire recording back to the patients so they could hear the engaged feedback and questions from the outside world. So each taping session at El Borda now started with listening instead of just having the patients start talking. This became a valuable therapeutic skill for isolated mental patients to master.

When a caller suggested creating a name for the radio broadcast, the topic intuitively called for community involvement and listener engagement—an interactive deliberation between the patients and the community. Of the forty names nominated, *La Colifata*, an affectionate way of referring to madness as "gone crazy," was finally decided on by the patients themselves. From then on what motivated this project were the listeners, who began to phone in and who started to listen intently to the sometimes bizarre but surprisingly often profound comments from people they thought were hopeless. From there, the most interesting aspects of *La Colifata* have been the therapeutic impact on the patients and also, and maybe of equal importance, the social and community mobilization that developed around the experience.

Undramatizing Without Denying

The problem with mental illness is that it is so complex and has so many variables that one interventionist, expert, or specialist is often not enough to provide satisfactory help. And at El Borda, with resources so limited, the patients couldn't get that sort of collective help in any event. But as the community started to get involved with the patients, the design of the show permitted anyone—a butcher, a farmer, or an auto mechanic—to help construct the program by interacting and intervening. They all added their unique perspectives. They could improve it, enrich it, and therefore affect its evolution to the point that their involvement formed an integral part of the project in and of itself. The show as well as the community of listeners and patients became transformed by everyone's total and open involvement.

The spontaneous action of the audience and the ability of both the audience and the patients to make space for each other continually altered and evolved the program. Soon, individuals and groups of listeners started to ask how they could collaborate above and beyond just listening and talking. They began to donate all sorts of useful items, including a small broadcast team, radio equipment, and an antenna to allow production of a real radio program instead of the audio clips that were being disseminated to participating radio stations. Other gifts included an old car (named "the first crazy mobile unit"), which necessitated that residents get permission to venture outside the walls of the hospital to broadcast. A unique gift was donated by an entire community in one area of Buenos Aires: a "free vacation" in another part of the city so patients could experience life outside El Borda. The inmates were so overwhelmed by this kindness and openness that they decided to give back to the community and started to use the "crazy mobile unit" to gather items that they could then donate to an organization in that community that supported street kids.

Each one of the listener offerings provided the patients and the community with another level of acceptance that was mutually reinforcing and life changing. A microsociety was being constructed by everyone involved, and it was changing the relationships between people. Audience and presenters were no longer at the level of sane and the sick, but rather at a level of connection and recognition of necessities, capabilities, and potential. And these newly formed relationships, though limited at that time to the Buenos Aires community, pointed toward a much larger way to help change relationships in a similar way around the world.

Former patient Hugo Lopez, who became a veteran presenter in the show while at El Borda, has now helped set up similar projects in Italy and Spain: "Our final goal is to rid the world of nut-houses. You should know that people on the outside are just as crazy as us loonies in here."[1]

Music with a Message

What *La Colifata* really intends to do is bring out the potential of others. Those who take part on both sides of the radio program now understand how participation has transformed them. This methodology has many aspects that can be useful for similar projects with different populations dealing with different issues—all leveraging dialogue with sectors of a community that tend to be excluded, segregated, or marginalized. Today, technology makes it much easier to create a radio-type show that incorporates the voices of differently abled people and identifies and appreciates the creation of a space where being different is an asset and not a boundary.

Since its inception, *La Colifata* has gained an ever-increasing fan base around the world. More than fifty "Station Colifatas" worldwide now broadcast the program or similar ventures from the original Argentine base to listeners in Spain, Germany, France, Italy, Chile, Uruguay, and Mexico. *La Colifata* was featured in the 2009 movie *Tetro*, directed by Francis Ford Coppola, and the patients recorded an album at the hospital with the famous European singer Manu Chao. Two years later, *La Colifata* participated in an album with the popular Spanish group El Canto del Loco. (The musicians were so enamored of the program and the participants that their disc not only has the patients from *La Colifata* introducing the songs, it also includes a documentary DVD about *La Colifata* that explains the complexities and meaning of the program.)[2]

A poignant example of the show's impact comes from Spain. The audience for El Canto del Loco in Spain consists of teenagers and young adults, mostly from fifteen to twenty years old. One of them was an eighteen-year-old who called in to the Spanish show. After buying the El Canto del Loco disc, he described an encounter with his neighbor from the second floor. Because the neighbor often talked to himself, the caller had never bothered to speak to him and rather avoided him. But after hearing the album and learning about *La Colifata* the eighteen-year-old asked his neighbor a question for the first time. Before the young man listened to the album, Alfredo reflects, "There were certainties built in his head that didn't allow for him to perceive the world in a different way. He opened up to questioning those certainties because of connecting to the reality of *La Colifata*." Like the young Spanish listener, audiences around the world have had their consciousness raised by the show's departure from the conventional radio show format and by its dynamic message. Now, both the radio program and the model it created have spawned hundreds of replications among a variety of populations for a multiplicity of issues.

In 2010, after talking about *La Colifata* at a conference in Germany, Alfredo realized that his work really does make a difference:

> *It had to do with something very simple which is that this group of people celebrated the liberty of speaking and expressing themselves and that there were others who listened to them. Neither the speakers nor the listeners were aware of the others' existence before this program. To celebrate the power to speak and be heard is very basic but so impactful at the same time. And now the methodology is legitimated as a psychological practice and it's slowly validated.*

The communication mechanism of *La Colifata* became a catalyst that created a space to highlight the random, the desperate, and the dormant potential of every single person involved, whether by producing, presenting, or listening. It helped create a reality that had not existed before by making everyone involved a protagonist. It created change by making room for everyone to be a changemaker.

Alfredo knows that *La Colifata* has done more than change him over the years; it has now become a part of him. He gave birth to this creation but he feels that the best thing that could happen would be for it to stop being his and become significant in our culture. Like many other social entrepreneurs he has learned that he has built something that is not only his but something for the entire world to enjoy and learn from.

On April 20, 2011, *La Colifata* passed its twentieth year. To celebrate, it can be heard live for the first time around the world through the Internet, along with twenty years of shows and audio clips streaming twenty-four hours a day at www.lacolifata.org.

PART 5

Cultivating Empathy

How we relate to others has a lot to do with what behaviors we see, what we experience, and how we perceive and interpret the environment that surrounds us. As the world is forced to open its eyes to increased violence and aggressive behavior from the youngest children to the oldest nations, two questions cry out for attention. What is fueling this closed-minded and aggressive (both physical and psychological) behavior? How can we deactivate the anger, the hatred, and the violence, and instill, develop, and build tolerance in each person for "the others" that carries forth over generations?

Lack of acceptance and understanding for the lives and emotions of others and unwillingness to accept the differences between ourselves and our neighbors are sadly getting to be commonplace, whether fueled by religious intolerance, governmental aggression, extreme poverty, or other incendiary conditions. Anyone can name a million causes, but how many can name even one solution? After you read this section, you'll be able to name at least three. As the saying goes, "The enemy is the difference between two perspectives and the ignorance between them."

REFLECTIONS BY
ARIANNA HUFFINGTON

"The ability to identify with another person's feelings." That is how Mary Gordon's organization, Roots of Empathy (whose good works are featured later in this part of the book), defines the elemental but elusive human quality that gives the group its name.

Empathy is a simple concept, which is actually why it has such potential to change the world. Last year, I became captivated by Jeremy Rifkin's book *The Empathic Civilization*, in which he explains that empathy is not a quaint behavior to be trotted out during intermittent holiday visits to a food bank or during a post-disaster telethon. Instead, it lies at the very core of human existence.

What Rifkin articulates—and backs up with scientific evidence—is something I've long believed. Indeed, I wrote a book dedicated to exploring what I called the Fourth Instinct—the instinct that compels us to go beyond our impulses for survival, sex, and power and drives us to expand the boundaries of our caring to include our communities and the world around us.

And in the years since I wrote my book, the role empathy plays in our lives has only grown more important. In fact, in this time of economic hardship, political instability, and rapid technological change, empathy is the one quality we most need if we're going to survive and flourish in the twenty-first century.

Just before he died, Jonas Salk defined the transitional period we're in as moving from Epoch A (based on survival and competition) to Epoch B (based on collaboration and meaning). And technological advances, including the advent of social media, have enabled us to collaborate in ways that would have been unimaginable only a decade ago. As Biz Stone, Twitter's co-founder, puts it, "Twitter is not a triumph of tech; it's a triumph of humanity."

When people used to offer to join Mother Teresa in her work with the needy of Calcutta, she would often respond: "Find your own Calcutta." That is, care for those in need where you are. Thousands are doing this, all across America, in ways that illustrate and even amplify the possibilities of Salk's Epoch B.

People like Eric Jirgens, an interior designer in Detroit who found himself getting a lot fewer jobs than he used to in his recession-ravaged city. So he put his underutilized skills to work transforming a women's shelter into a beautiful and more welcoming space for the women who have to temporarily call it home.

And Jacqueline Novogratz, who, as head of the Acumen Fund, has combined her expertise in finance with her gift for empathy, investing from Kenya to Karachi and Dubai in start-ups that help improve the lives of those unable to do so on their own.

And Cheryl Jacobs, who along with her work as a torts lawyer at a big firm had been doing pro bono work with the highly successful Residential Mortgage Foreclosure Diversion Program in Philadelphia, which helps homeowners facing foreclosure navigate the legal process. After being laid off, Jacobs took on even more foreclosure cases, eventually opening her own practice dedicated to helping people keep their homes.

I have been lucky enough, in the course of my travels around the country and around the world, to meet and work with many people who have bolstered my faith in our collective ability to confront the crises we face. And I am increasingly convinced that the solutions to our problems are not going to come from the political, media, and financial institutions that continue to fail us.

The solutions are going to come from each of us doing our part—making a personal commitment and taking action. And to summon our better angels, there are two essential ingredients we'll need: innovation nurtured by an entrepreneurial spirit, and empathy nurtured by a strong civil society. The individuals and organizations described in the following chapters are inspiring illustrations of both. They have mastered the gift of identifying with other people's feelings.

In spite of the challenges ahead, when I read their stories I am reminded of the combustible creativity that results when empathy meets imagination, and I am filled with hope.

Arianna Huffington is an author and syndicated columnist. She is co-founder of the news website *The Huffington Post* and in 2009 was named to *Forbes* list of the most influential women in media.

CHAPTER 16

From Babies to Behavioral Shift—Canada

Mary Gordon created the Roots of Empathy program in 1996 with the goal of building caring, peaceful, and civil societies in the next generation by fostering empathy in children. Her innovation leverages the interactions between a parent and infant by bringing them into the classroom as an ideal model of empathy from which children can learn.

THE ROOTS OF EMPATHY GREEN BLANKET WAS SPREAD ON THE FLOOR of the classroom. A mother and her tiny four-month-old baby entered the room and all the children stood around the blanket in a circle while quietly singing the Roots of Empathy Welcome song. As she slowly walked around the inside of the circle, the mother held her daughter in front of her at the children's eye level, so that every child had a chance to connect lovingly with the baby. The children soothingly repeated the same song as the baby went around, and it seemed as if every child was being emotionally touched by the experience.

This same scene plays out with children in every Roots of Empathy program around the world. A Roots of Empathy family visit always starts with the Welcome song. And whether children are singing in Cree or in French or in English, it's always the same tune, same format, and same program. They aren't aware of it, but the experience is being biologically embedded in their brains.

After the Welcome song, the class sits down around the green blanket. The mother also sits and gently places her child before her. In the middle, the baby seems vulnerable, but not threatened or threatening. Guided by a trained Roots of Empathy instructor, the children learn to observe the baby carefully. Slowly, surely, and miraculously, the children find the humanity in the baby by coming to understand that baby's intentions and feelings. Babies do not hide their feelings; they have no screens or filters. You can always tell when a baby has a problem. Lacking words, a baby emotes with vocalizations and movements, which Gordon describes as a "theatre of emotion." As the children begin to understand a baby's language of feelings, they start to name those feelings. Then they are guided by the instructor to understand and name their own feelings and the feelings of others—the very definition of empathy. By finding the humanity in the baby, they learn to find it in themselves and each other. They learn that we all share the same feelings—this is our common language, our first language; it is the foundation for our shared humanity.

The year-long Roots of Empathy program is demonstrating a new way to relate to other human beings. The program is predicated on the notion that while schools are responsible for what children know, Roots of Empathy gets at what they feel and what they think, through direct, experiential learning about empathy. And that's the difference. Every child sitting around that blanket is very much transformed. Those children who didn't grow up with a loving attachment relationship in their lives may not know much about how love works, but as of this day forward, they will not forget. A new pathway has been created in their brains.

And throughout the rest of the program, they'll have this pathway strengthened. As Mary explains:

> In your first eighteen months of life, you decide if you are lovable or not, if you deserve to be taken care of, if you're worthy. If you figure out that the only people you love can't always be depended on, it's going to be a problem. So parents become the most important people in determining how the baby feels in the world and how they grow emotionally. Just by loving the child, the child responds. That's how they learn the human language. They don't need Berlitz, they need love.

And that foundation of love is the inspiration behind Roots of Empathy.

Empathy Can't Be Taught, But It Can Be Caught

The Roots of Empathy program is designed for children ages five to thirteen and offered in classrooms from kindergarten up to Grade 8. Mary started the program more than fifteen years ago, and to this day parents still ask her if it is ever too late for a child to develop empathy. She often answers by telling the story of Darren, who saw his mother murdered in front of him when he was four. Since then, he had been in and out of foster care situations and was held back twice in school. His tattoo and shaved head made him look menacing, and he was two years older than anyone else in his eighth-grade class, which was receiving the Roots of Empathy program.

During class one day, the volunteer Roots of Empathy mother was explaining that whenever she put her baby in a Snugli (a cloth carrier to hold a baby close to the chest), her baby wouldn't snuggle in and face her, and only tolerated it when facing outwards. As the bell rang and most of the kids were leaving to go to lunch, the mother asked if anyone would like to try on the Snugli. To everyone's surprise, Darren volunteered. He ever so gently put the baby in the Snugli, chest to chest. The baby molded completely into him, something the mother had just explained she couldn't do with her child. Darren took the baby into the corner and started to rock back and forth. A few minutes later as he gave the baby back, he asked the Roots of Empathy instructor, "Do you think if no one has ever loved you, you could still be a good father?" For the first time he believed in the possibility that maybe he, too, could be a loving parent, even though he had experienced very little love in life himself.

For Mary, this story told her never to give up on anyone. She often says that empathy can't be taught, but she is adamant that it can be caught—developed through experiencing it, as Darren did by witnessing the empathy that the mother had shown for the baby in his classroom and later by coming to understand the baby's feelings and feel love for the baby himself. Roots of Empathy is built on the certainty that we are all born with the capacity for empathy, but we need to experience it to more fully develop that capacity as we age. When children experience empathy for "their" baby, it gives them a foundation for life that will help them grow into more empathetic people, friends, parents, and citizens down the road.

Developing Emotional Fluency

The experience around the Roots of Empathy green blanket is a platform, a springboard that helps children dive into their own emotions and feelings. After discussing why the baby might be feeling happy, excited, worried, anxious, or angry, the instructor then uses those feelings to reference the children's lived experience. *When was a time that you felt frustrated like our baby? What did you do about it? When was a time that you felt so angry that you cried like the baby? Who did you tell and how did you cope and how did you know you were angry?* The discussion turns ever inward. *When did you feel like that? How can you tell when others feel that way?* As the children share their experiences and reflections on feelings, they come to realize that their deepest emotions are shared by others and they are not so different after all. The program builds the children's emotional literacy; it builds their coping strategies, augments their self-knowledge and shows them ways to self-regulate. It connects them, each to the other.

Mary often says that we live in an emotionally illiterate society, particularly in North America. It is no wonder that many children don't know what their feelings are, let alone how to describe them or manage them.

Throughout the year, the children watch the baby grow and develop. Each predictable developmental stage that the baby goes through and each milestone in the baby's life adds to the range of emotions that children observe. For example, when babies crawl for the first time, children observe how proud they are of their new skill, and then have a chance to reflect on a time they learned to do something new. They learn to feel proud of the fact that once they couldn't do many things like their babies—perhaps riding a bike, jumping rope, or reading a book—but now they can. And they come to realize there may be other things they can't do yet—but they will learn to do them eventually, just like their baby.

Roots of Empathy also builds on the fact that babies display different reactions and emotions according to their unique temperaments. For example, it may turn out that a particular baby is easily frustrated and cries often. This can be a powerful lesson. In Roots of Empathy, children learn to identify a baby's temperament and reflect on what their own temperament is like. They learn about individual differences, and that it is okay to have a temperament that is distinct from others as it is important to understand and accept people with temperaments different from their own. A Roots of Empathy instructor might get children thinking about ways to help a more cautious baby feel better, such as introducing new things slowly or bringing him to his mother for comfort if he is truly overwhelmed and having a hard time adjusting to a new environment. All this intensifies the richness of the discussions and the impact of the program on children's emotional literacy.

How We Feel Is Who We Are

Mary often explains emotional literacy to educators by asking a traditional question from the world of academia. "If Johnny has three apples and Amelia takes two, how many are left?" The Roots of Empathy program asks the question entirely differently: "If Johnny has three apples and Amelia takes two, how is Johnny going to feel?" Mary notes that how Johnny feels is going to determine everything he learns that day—or not. Roots of Empathy proposes that if we can use the universal access point of public education in developed countries to raise levels of empathy and increase the social and emotional learning of children, we can have a ripple effect in almost every single measureable outcome of societal wellness—from criminal activity, unemployment, addiction, poor parenting, and family violence to civic participation and mental health. The research on social and emotional learning clearly states that when children have a better understanding of their own emotions and a greater sense of connection with others, their academic performance improves, and so does their success and happiness in later life.

Research on Roots of Empathy clearly shows that the program is making a large contribution to children's social and emotional learning. For more than a decade, independent researchers worldwide have been studying the program, and have consistently found that Roots of Empathy significantly reduces aggression (including bullying) and increases pro-social behavior (such as sharing, including, and cooperating) among children who receive it. The effects of the program have even been shown to last at least three years, in the longest study of program benefits that has been conducted to date.

Now research into the program is taking a new turn. At the University of Washington's Institute for Learning and Brain Sciences (I-LABS), Drs. Andrew Meltzoff and Patricia Kuhl are conducting a brain-based study of the program in Seattle, using state-of-the-art, noninvasive MEG imaging technology to measure activity in different parts of children's brains. Using this technology, they will be able to show whether the program has a biological effect on key indicators of social-emotional competency, such as increased activity in areas of the brain that indicate the ability to regulate emotions. It will be one of the first neurophysiological studies ever to measure the effects of a social and emotional learning program on a child's brain, with results expected in 2013.

We Need a Global Warming of Our Hearts

Roots of Empathy encourages children to be fixers or changers. If they see someone being cruel or unkind in the classroom or on the playground, they have an opportunity to stand up against it. The program instills the "everyone a changemaker" attitude by operating on the principle of participatory democracy. There is no praise for a right answer in a Roots of Empathy program—in fact, there are no right or wrong answers in the program at all, just children sharing their thoughts and feelings. Children are always acknowledged and thanked for their contribution to the group discussion, and therefore know that they are being heard. "If a child gets to hear that their voice counts in grade one, can you imagine how powerfully they can grow as citizens? And as changemakers?" Mary asks. The participatory democracy approach also builds children's intrinsic motivation. They contribute not to be rewarded by praise, but because they want to share in the discussion. And what is most amazing is that as they go through the program they do grow as changemakers.

Mary tells a story of a class of nine-year-old children lining up to go out to recess. When the teacher wasn't looking, one boy grabbed another boy's hat. The smallest little girl in the class looked at the boy who had grabbed the hat, and told him as calmly and powerfully as she could to give back the hat. He looked up and down the row of children and by their silence and the look on their faces, he realized that the moral majority was on her side. In most classrooms, no one would have said anything. In this case, the bully learned that his game was not going to work because there were children in his class who cared about how other children feel and were willing to stand up for it. Better yet, he learned that if he did similar things in future, he was going to be the one who would be embarrassed. The ecology of the class was now forever tipped. Mary knows hundreds of stories that play out like this one.

Dismantling the "Other"

Mary looks at the world and thinks about what the nature of a citizen is and what we need to do to build a more civil society. She created Roots of Empathy's mission around building a more caring, peaceful, and civil society by raising levels of empathy in children and adults. She passionately believes that we can increase children's empathy quotient and decrease their aggression toward others. If she can effect that sort of change in society, then people will find it difficult to dehumanize or turn their backs on others. Our world today offers lots of examples of people who propagate cruelty, who decide that if others are different in some way or believe in different things, they have the right to marginalize them. But when you introduce empathy to the picture, it is much harder to believe others are so different from ourselves. Roots of Empathy helps children intentionally identify how we are different but also how we are the same.

> *I am convinced that one of the biggest things we need to do to change the world is erase the concept of "the other." In order to be successful, we have to do more than secure economic prosperity; we will wither and fail as a society unless we become empathetic. We may be divided by any number of differences—geography, culture, race, class, age, ability, sexual orientation or gender—but we are all connected by shared emotions.*

Using the baby makes it easy to explain that we are all different in some ways, but that doesn't make us good or bad, she adds. It means we recognize the differences and value them rather than marginalize them. Our feelings are what ultimately connects us as human beings. And empathy, one of the most important human traits, is what allows us to connect to each other.

Creating an Empathy Movement

Roots of Empathy's aim is to change the world, child by child, and the program is now spreading widely and internationally. So far, about four hundred thousand children worldwide have received Roots of Empathy's programs in seven countries. The program has a large reach across Canada where it began, but it is also growing in the United States, Northern Ireland, the Republic of Ireland, the Isle of Man, Scotland, and New Zealand. Roots of Empathy received a 2011 Globalizer Award from Ashoka, which is helping the organization to further increase its reach in a sustainable way, internationally. But perhaps the most important thing that Roots of Empathy is doing is leading by example, influencing the world's thought leaders, social entrepreneurs, and humanitarians by demonstrating the difference empathy makes to our global well-being. In 2010, Mary was asked to speak about emotional literacy as part of the United Nations' International Literacy Day celebrations. It was the first time the concept of emotional literacy had been included at the event.

What Roots of Empathy has helped to launch is a world empathy movement that aims to create a shift in education—and beyond—so that empathy is nurtured as the most important trait we need to create an "everyone a changemaker" world. "It's about creating a more humane world," says Mary. "This is about the human family—we all share this world together. But it is only through empathy that we'll be able to solve the world's problems."

CHAPTER 17

Cultivating Champions of Interfaith Action—United States

Eboo Patel is pioneering a market for interfaith action by cultivating leaders among religiously diverse students on college campuses. His goal is a global movement of understanding, cooperation, and action with college and university campuses at the center. He is the founder and president of Interfaith Youth Core.

Who did you feed in Ramallah by not talking to Hillel? Who did you keep safe in the south of Israel by not talking to the Muslim Students' Association?

—EBOO PATEL

RELIGION IS A POWERFUL FORCE IN THE WORLD. IT CAN DIVIDE US, causing painful and long-lasting conflicts, or it can help unite us. No surprise here. Too often, we hear the noise made by religious extremists and not the voices of the people who are united against them. Prejudice, ignorance, and violence among people of different religions feel widespread. Eboo Patel believes the solution is building sustainable understanding and cooperation between diverse religious populations.

Building a Core of Campus Champions

Eboo is passionately certain that the solution is not a program that will fall from Heaven, nor a methodology written in a book. It's about having enough interfaith leaders and champions of interfaith action who have learned the methodology of building and strengthening ties across religions and who can attract a large number of committed people to that cause. For Eboo, it's always about people. And not just about a few people here and there, running a program with a few like-minded individuals. It's got to be about involving enough people to form a tipping point. Enough people who, when connected together, become a movement.

Martin Luther King Jr. was twenty-six when he organized the Montgomery Bus Boycott, and Gandhi was in his twenties when he began his peace-building work in South Africa. Jane Addams, the woman Eboo feels exemplifies citizens who build institutions to meet the challenge of their era, started Hull House (America's first homeless shelter) when she was in her late twenties. As we have seen in the past and again through the 2011 "Arab Spring" uprisings across North Africa, it is often the shoes of young people that leave the largest transformational footprints.

Eboo Patel was twenty-two when he created the Interfaith Youth Core (IFYC), and his trajectory is following a similar path to those mentioned above. Growing up as an Indian-born Muslim in Chicago, his early life was rife with racism, religious prejudice, and rejection. Having been a victim of religious intolerance, it would have been natural for Eboo to take one of two paths in life: to question why religion causes such viciousness and violence around the world, or to become an intolerant bully himself. He asked himself what would set him apart.

Putting Faith in Interfaith

Eboo's core belief is that religion can and should be a bridge of cooperation rather than a barrier of division. His Muslim faith, his Indian heritage, and his American upbringing have given rise to his bridge-building mission. So it often pained him to read or listen to the daily news because it seemed as if religious bigotry and the resulting conflicts were the main headline. Where was the other side of the story? Where were the people of different faiths and traditions who were working together to promote the common good? They must be somewhere—but there didn't seem to be enough of them to really make a difference. These questions inspired the creation of the Interfaith Youth Core and led to two solution-oriented thoughts: what if people of all faiths and no faith worked together to change the world, and what if students led this charge and campuses became the ground for a global movement of interfaith cooperation? What if we could prove that the twenty-first century can be defined by cooperation between diverse communities instead of conflict?

Eboo's defining moment came in college in 1995. A professor handed him a copy of an article by David Bornstein about Mohammed Yunus, who created the microfinance movement.[1]

I became fully interested in this guy who was at the center of a terrible system of poverty surrounding the worth of labor in Bangladesh and managed to see that the inherent social problem was access to capital. Instead of writing a book about it or starting a charity, he started a whole new system of finance to get capital to women in villages. He was a social entrepreneur. Well, I'd sit around dreaming of new solutions to social problems, but I thought the only career path open to me was being a professor, and all I'd ever be able to do was write about those ideas. But here was a person who was making a career out of solving problems in a pattern-changing way. That changed my life. I realized that is who I could be—not a professor but a social entrepreneur. I called that my moment of having an identity of a social entrepreneur. Consequently what we try to do at the Interfaith Youth Core is articulate the identity of an interfaith leader and then—following the path of Yunus—we say, "Listen, there's a problem in the world that we have to solve."

Enhancing Your Religion Through Exposure to Others

IFYC was created to implement answers to Eboo's questions. Started in 1998 and incorporated in 2002, it began with the help of a Jewish friend of Eboo's and an Evangelical Christian employee. By late 2011, it had grown into a staff of thirty-five with a $4 million budget. It's always been centered around one crucial idea: Have students of different backgrounds, from different walks of life and religions, bridge the divide by working together in the service of others, learning about themselves through feeding the poor, working in a homeless shelter, or painting schools. From the beginning, service learning was to be the bridge that would lead to the creation of interfaith dialogue on a grand scale, eventually feeding a movement. Service learning and a focus on shared values continue as core methodologies for IFYC programs today.

One of the other methodologies that has since become core is bridging off current events, which have given the idea of IFYC a real boost that could not have been anticipated. Consider the election of U.S. President Barack Obama. IFYC used the president's history as a community organizer in Chicago working with Protestant churches, Catholic churches, and Muslim communities under the tutelage of a Jewish mentor to relate to the model that IFYC wants to spread. The story of the proposed mosque near Ground Zero in New York City, and the ugly discourse that surrounded it, provided a real lesson around the role of religious prejudice in our society and helped articulate the Interfaith Youth Core as an alternative and a solution. For Eboo, current events are opportunities to continually highlight the relevance of the IFYC message and to grow its existing programs. He sees them as just another way to build a society characterized by understanding and cooperation between people from different religious communities.

At the beginning, it was current events that had led Eboo to reason that "if Muslim radicals and extremists of other religions were recruiting young people, then those who believe in religious tolerance should also enlist the youth."[2] So he started to focus on college campuses where interfaith advocacy could take the form of activism. He figured that it could become a norm, much as women's rights now were in some parts of the world, and it could be as ambitious as Teach for America (a U.S. program committed to educational equity and excellence that has become one of the nation's largest providers of teachers for low-income communities).

New Voices and Visions

In Eboo's mind, the only way to overcome destructive religious fanaticism is to create communities where human connection transcends differences of race, religion, and culture. He once told National Public Radio, "I recognize now that believing in pluralism means having the courage to act on it. In other words, action is what separates belief from merely an opinion."[3]

Eboo defines IFYC's product as threefold. First is the message of interfaith cooperation. Second are the college campuses that articulate interfaith cooperation as a high priority. And third are the young people who see themselves as interfaith leaders and want to start interfaith cooperation projects. Cultivating these future interfaith leaders is one of Eboo's top priorities as they will be the backbone of the movement, the changemakers of tomorrow.

The hurdle is, it's not easy to find those young people. As Eboo explains it, part of the difficulty relates to the way that our education system trains people for certain professions; if you want to hire them you go to the specific type of school that trains them. If you go to medical school to become a doctor, obviously hospitals will go to medical schools to hire doctors. If you go to law school to become a lawyer, obviously law firms will go to law schools for new hires. If you are recruiting for McKinsey, you can go practically anywhere—every business school in America is training people to become McKinsey consultants.

The point is, there is a pipeline of talent coming into these institutions. But there is no pipeline of trained talent for interfaith leadership. People may have content knowledge from seminaries or from masters' programs in religion, but in the end, interfaith leadership is not just a matter of having the right content knowledge; it also requires demonstrating the ability to mobilize, organize, and inspire others and make a difference on a large scale. If new voices and visions are the products of IFYC, it is producing them by pioneering a market for interfaith action.

"Better Together"

"Better Together" is a good example of such pioneering. It's a year-long campaign led by college students who want to take a stand for interfaith cooperation. The campaign has three goals: to empower students to lead activities that build interfaith cooperation on campus; to equip campuses to become places where a critical mass of students participate in interfaith action and conversation; and to spark a global movement of interfaith cooperation with college and university campuses at the center.

The campaign is also a way of training interfaith leaders who can mobilize, organize, and be the leaders of tomorrow. Joshua Stanton, who was an undergraduate at Amherst when he spent a year in formal training with IFYC, writes:[4]

> I went from seeing interfaith work as a hobby to realizing it as a calling. I was a committed Jew, pursuing the possibility of ordination as a rabbi after college. In the year I spent working intensively with the Interfaith Youth Core, I realized that I couldn't be an effective religious leader in a religiously diverse country unless I robustly engaged with leaders—and congregants—of other traditions. I also realized that seminary education did not always provide a space for students and professors to study the differences between religious traditions in a way that led to productive strategies for interfaith engagement, or even clarity about the nature of the differences themselves. So, when I was a first-year rabbinical student, I founded a peer-reviewed academic journal and online forum, the *Journal of Inter-Religious Dialogue*, to bring tough issues into the open and enable scholars, clergy, students, and non-profit leaders to

engage with each other. The Interfaith Youth Core taught me how to transform an environment, such that our over 120,000 yearly readers and contributors from across traditions and institutions now have a space in which to guide their interfaith work with rigorous thought, dialogue, and personal discernment.

Seeing Similarities, Not Differences

Eboo would love to see interfaith cooperation become a social norm, just the way sustainability has become.

Thirty years ago protecting the environment wasn't a social norm, but right now, when we are done with our coffee, we will look for a recycling container. We have an internal social-cultural expectation of what we should do with a plastic or paper cup and we expect the business that we are buying it from to meet that expectation. That is what a social norm is. The same with social entrepreneurship—it too is on its way to becoming a social norm. People know what it means, they talk about it, people aspire to work in that field, it carries a sense of value. That is where I want to see the interfaith movement in ten years. In ten years, I want every college campus to have an interfaith program, just like you'd have a multicultural program, just like you'd have service days.

The future Eboo envisions doesn't stop there. His concept is huge and inspirational, but amazingly practicable at the same time:

I'd like those programs to be consistent with what we think of as the excellence of the Interfaith Youth Core: programs that are capable of turning our civil society around. College interfaith programs that have a chance to make a difference are ones that are led by small groups of students and involve large groups of students, where the college president should be able to shake the hand of his or her graduates and have a reasonable degree of confidence that those graduates have acquired interfaith literacy, have engaged in interfaith service, and have acquired interfaith leadership over their four years at that institution of higher education.

A population disconnected from parts of itself will not fight to protect the freedoms of all. It seems like a logical imperative to increase understanding between religions and nonreligious people to bridge the divide between people with different worldviews. In the face of national and global religious strife, it's time to take a stand for cooperation and prove that we are better together. Eboo believes that faith in the twenty-first century can build bridges of cooperation that are stronger than barriers of division. Once he gets the United States in shape, he will turn to the rest of the world.

Amen. Sign me up.

CHAPTER 18

Beautiful Resistance— Palestine

Abdelfattah Abusrour created Alrowwad, a place to help children and women experience normalcy and to regain their inner human values while living in the middle of a conflict zone.

I want these children to grow up to be great changemakers so they can think that they can change the world without the need to carry a gun to kill anybody else in order to earn a living or to be alive. I want to help them hold on to their humanity and become role models to create a world where every day that comes is more beautiful than the day that goes before.

—ABDELFATTAH ABUSROUR

IN 1994, ABDELFATTAH ABUSROUR RETURNED TO PALESTINE AFTER nine years in France, where he had obtained his master's and PhD in biological and medical engineering. As a Palestinian, he'd been following the situation there, and what he learned choked his nationalistic pride and strained his love of peace for his fellow countrymen and women. It especially tore him apart to think of the way the children were suffering amid the difficulties they were having since the Israeli occupation. He intuitively knew that he could make more of a change on the ground than behind a desk in his "underground scientific palace."

When he could no longer deny that his passion for his country was stronger than his need to live a comfortable life in Paris, he decided to return to Palestine. But not just anywhere in Palestine—he moved to the place where he'd grown up: the Aida Refugee Camp in Bethlehem. He returned to his roots to see if he could help the children who now lived there and were following in his childhood footsteps. He found work as an assistant professor at two universities while simultaneously working as a researcher in genetic engineering and the head of biologic analysis for a pharmaceutical company in Beit Jala, Palestine. He loved his work and was ambitious and as a result worked seven days a week in three different locations. In addition, he volunteered to teach theater at one of the universities, in the schools of the camp, and wherever he was asked to volunteer.

Interests Change, Values Endure

In Palestine, Abdelfattah observed despair and sadness. He witnessed anger and violence. He listened to cries of revenge and hatred. But he was most disturbed when he looked in his own children's eyes and thought about the heritage he and others would be leaving for them. And though a lot of people said that the situation in Palestine was a political nightmare, a desperate state of affairs with little they could do, he knew that no Palestinian had the luxury of despair. That was not going to be a legacy that anybody could be proud to leave their children and the generations to come. What he needed to do was to lift the heaviness of ill will that was crushing the Palestinian spirit and cultivate the values that he grew up appreciating: justice, freedom, love, and peace; values that should be shared by every human being. Abdelfattah is a firm believer in a consistent set of values for all humanity:

> *These values we share—whether we are Muslim or Christian, Jewish or Buddhist, Hindu or atheist, or whatever we are—they are not elastic. They do not change based on new realities on the ground or the dictation of one leader or one country or another. They are the essential flower of humanity and the cultural heritage we want to leave all of our children for generations to come. It's to the commitment to these values, the defense of these values, the protection of our humanity and pride in our heritage that we will leave behind; that is what my work is all about.*

He wanted to bring the beauty back in people's hearts. He wanted to see it reflecting back in their eyes. He didn't want people to grow up thinking that the only way of resistance is throwing stones and burning tires, whether out of anger or boredom because the schools were closed. He wanted to "provide a safe space where children and youth can show their beauty and humanity through arts and narrate their stories through 'Beautiful Resistance' against the ugliness of occupation and violence."

Beautiful Resistance became his mission, and in 1998, he created Alrowwad (Pioneers for Life) as both a physical and an emotional space where children and adults could come to express their feelings through the arts—in music, photography, painting, and theater. Alrowwad became a community center, a safe and positive space for children and women, who are the main focus of the program. Abdelfattah's vision was to create an empowered Palestinian society through educational and artistic means, a society free of violence, respectful of human rights and values, and based on the spirit of social entrepreneurship, innovation, and self-expression.

It was critical for people to look at this Beautiful Resistance as builders for future generations. And this is an act of resistance because, yes, we are not compromising our story or our narratives but are trying to remain truthful and integral to the values we share without being hypocritical about them.

Beauty and the Beast Within

What is truly amazing is that Abdelfattah created Alrowwad and his antiviolence program after the first Palestinian intifada, the popular uprising against Israel from 1989–1993, and two years before the second intifada, from 2000–2005. He was able to continue and grow it throughout a very tense time both within and outside Palestine. Starting out in Abdelfattah's brother's house, and his parents', moving from a two-room space into a three-story building, Alrowwad has continued to work out of its base in the Aida camp. It now has room for many different groups, and has expanded its services via a mobile program (Mobile Beautiful Resistance) that brings activities to different cities that have been deprived of visits from artistic troupes or lack facilities for the arts or libraries or outdoor games.

But as the program grew, so did the need for it. The situation in the Aida camp changed drastically after the wall of separation was erected, bringing with it rising unemployment rates and escalating land costs. With the construction of the wall, open spaces where the children used to play were lost. Except for places like Alrowwad most children had nothing but the street to play in. They had no place to pass their time, to experience childhood, and to express their inner anxieties and tensions. Many of the children had suffered deeply; they had seen their own houses and the houses of their neighbors destroyed, they had seen people killed, and some had seen their own parents or siblings dying in front of them.

One of them, a girl named Woud who came from a village named Ajjour, saw her mother die before her eyes after Israeli soldiers broke down the door of her house while her mother was standing behind it. Luckily she found Alrowwad and after three years was finally able to talk about the story of her mother's death. Her words sum up the impact of the program on children's lives and hearts. "I am using this Beautiful Resistance to express myself and tell my story eventually, but also to talk to the beast within me, before talking to the beasts of others." The change in Woud was dramatic and as she entered her first year of pharmacy school, she became even more of a role model for children similarly distressed.

Ribal lived in the house next door. He also witnessed many things that you always try to shield children from seeing or being part of. He has been in Alrowwad since 1998, when he was seven years old. In 2011 he graduated from the Faculty of Law of Alquds University in Palestine, with hopes of being a lawyer. For four years during his law studies, he was coordinator of the arts unit at Alrowwad and also coordinator of volunteers. He taught dance and has gone on tour with the Alrowwad traveling theater company in France, Belgium, the United States, Sweden, Denmark, Austria, and Luxembourg. He gives back by sharing his positive and energized self to others whenever and wherever he can.

Woud's and Ribal's stories reflect those of many other children who have grown up at Alrowwad. Thanks to its existence, they are now becoming the new face of Palestine.

Import, Export

When Abdelfattah returned to his homeland, he made a commitment to himself and his community to put the priority of the people before the priority of any political party. As he saw anger and armed resistance against Israel rising, he was surprised to see similar emotions and aggressive behavior playing out inside Palestine as well, between the major political parties. In a highly partisan culture, it became clear that to affiliate with a party might well lead toward a path to disputes and violence for both him and his children, so he determined that he needed to remain independent of any political party on a personal as well as organization level.

Remaining independent was not an easy thing to accomplish. Ultimately it meant that neither political side would ever give him money and support. So he developed a number of partnerships inside and outside Palestine to sustain the operations of the center along with a growing number of outreach programs within Palestine's borders. He started to create networks and "Friends of Alrowwad" organizations in France and worked on similar connections with nonprofits in the United States. His work quickly rippled out. Not long ago, four schools came to the Center from Norway looking for a partner to support in Palestine. The sixteen- to eighteen-year-old students—from a calm, mostly peaceful country—really had their eyes opened to the differences in how people live and to the changes they themselves might be able to make to help others in the world. They were deeply inspired to connect and committed to build their partnership with Alrowwad. This partnership became a blueprint for how Alrowwad could create future changemakers both in and outside of Palestine.

In 2010 alone, sixteen hundred people from about fifteen countries visited the Center in the Aida Refugee Camp. Some visitors were inspired to work with the Center; others were just thankful for the opportunity to meet with people who exemplified a spirit of hope. Many who visited connected with different issues or interests—sometimes environmental, sometimes political, humanistic, or artistic. But normally the biggest connection is made through Abdelfattah's passion for what he does and his way of making people feel responsible for their involvement in making change happen. He does not want to be seen as a humanitarian case, nor a case of charity or pity, so instead he involves people in the spirit of partnership. This type of relationship makes supporters feel part of what Alrowwad does, and they often come back annually to see what transpired over the year and what the future possibilities could be. Alrowwad has become a model program for children growing up in conflict zones anywhere in the world. As the story of the Center's impact circulates outside Palestine, replication will follow.

Many who come make a commitment to volunteer. It's a continuous relationship and partnership that goes beyond a funding issue. It's a commitment to something they feel part of, and their participation is as important for them as it is for the Center. Usually, people who are in solidarity with Palestine are from an older generation. So this is a great model where really young people can learn and understand the issue and get committed to a cause. After spending two days in Alrowwad, they see what the Center does, they stay among the young people, everyone works

230

together, and they all experience the possibilities for exchange. The emotional and intellectual connections affect everyone, and all feel that they are now part of a change that empowers action rather than overwhelms with despair and inertia. These intangible and unquantifiable sentiments propel students to see themselves as future world changemakers. As they mature they will hopefully commit themselves to the values that we share as human beings. Abdelfattah is hoping to export this model outside Palestine, so it can be duplicated; his vision is that this will go a long way to create a world where we won't deform our values to win an election or to please others around us, but we will elect or choose our leaders because they uphold those values that we treasure.

Conversely, when the Center's theater troupe performs its story in different places around the world, it often causes a dramatic learning experience for everyone. After a performance when the troupe recently visited the southern part of the United States, an African American student remarked that though she often complained that she couldn't do this or that where she lived, how can she now continue to complain when the Alrowwad kids live in a refugee camp and can hardly do anything that she can in the United States? In Paris, France, the troupe performed in the Eighteenth Arrondissement, a poor section of the city predominantly inhabited by foreigners. What a revelation when the kids from Palestine realized that the kids in Paris were poorer than they were!

Seeing how others are living, how others are struggling in different places, created much more impact in strengthening the idea that we are all human beings and we all share an equal part in making changes for each other. Abdelfattah hopes that these lessons will help everyone get beyond their own prisons, beyond their own realities, and see how connected they are to others around them. For Abdelfattah, that was the point at which he knew that the message finally reached his children—that there are different injustices in different countries, whether social, religious, or economic. This knowledge, he realized, unites everyone and inspires respect regardless of where someone lives, or their color or nationality.

Values Need to Surpass Violence

But for this to happen Abdelfattah knows that people's priorities have to become less superficial. They need to focus less on what football match they are watching, what concert they are going to, or who a celebrity marries (or divorces). He gets annoyed that when it comes to essential issues, very few people are thinking about them: "You will find millions in the streets when a football game is happening but for environmental issues, for attacks on culture, for lack of teachers or good schools, these valuable causes become secondary to the sport matches on television or radio." He wants people to start to focus more on these extremely important problems and rescue the future of humanity.

When Abdelfattah came back to Palestine in 1994, nonviolence was a totally unpopular concept because it was transmitted as a passive and negative action that involved normalization with Israelis. In those years, anything that sounded peaceful, and therefore potentially compromising, was not an acceptable stand for a Palestinian to make. It took quite a long time for Abdelfattah to explain that his way of resistance did not signify giving up or giving in—it was just a way to hold on to your values and beliefs and express them in "beautiful versus ugly ways." But the vision and passion for the legacy and spirit he was trying to kindle was far stronger than the mockery and accusations he had to endure. He dared not to fear being called a coward and passive. He held fast to his vision that Palestinians deserve their rights and their homeland,

and also to his belief that those cannot be obtained with violence and with the huge cost of losing a piece of your heart and soul to hatred. To his credit, just recently Abdelfattah has been hearing Palestinian political parties and even the prime minister talk about the importance of nonviolence being an acceptable part of popular resistance. He feels it's quite a breakthrough for people in positions of authority and political leadership to work toward helping the Palestinian people find peace within themselves and rekindle the inner beauty he fears they have been losing. The true long-lasting impact will be the change from the negative connotation of nonviolent resistance as passive and compromising to its positive meaning, which is in line with and integral to the noncompromised values of the people.

Anyone can slay a dragon . . . but try waking up every morning and loving the world all over again. That's what takes a real hero.

—BRIAN ANDREAS

Over the years, since Abdelfattah started Alrowwad and his Beautiful Resistance movement, he has become more aware of the importance and power of every individual and the extent to which he needs commitment from many individuals to make values surpass violence. He has become more convinced that there can be no compromises on human values. When he thinks about injustice, he is determined that a key part of his role as a changemaker is to be true to these values. This conviction has gotten him to think beyond his needs as a Palestinian to those he has as a universal human being.

Abdelfattah relates his favorite story:

There was a village which was about to suffer from hunger so the chief of the village asked everybody to come and say, well, we may have difficult months ahead, so what do you propose? Someone said, we can share. Everyone can contribute one liter of milk in a container in the center of the village so we can make cheese, we can make butter, we can make yogurt. So everybody was happy with the idea, and everybody agreed. All during the night people were pouring their liters in the big container. Next morning, they open the big container, and what do they find? They find only water in the container.

Everyone was thinking, if one puts one liter of water in all this milk, no one will notice. Everyone was thinking I don't have to do it, everyone else will do it. And they were mistaken, because everyone is responsible and I am saying every day I am going with my liter of milk to this big container. If you want to join in that's fine, if you don't, that's fine as well, but I will never go to this container with a liter of water. This is the commitment I have made after thirteen years of flirting with this Beautiful Resistance.

Abdelfattah knows that, like Woud, his people need to build peace within for themselves before they can build peace with others. His ultimate goal is to never hear people say, "We die, we die, so that Palestine lives," but instead to hear, "We live, we live, so that Palestine and every other country can live as well."

While the outcomes of our efforts may not be visible, work carried out with dignity and grace, ultimately produces more of the same.

—MARTIN LUTHER KING JR.

CHAPTER 19

Conclusion

Turning What Is and What If into What Can Be

Twenty years from now you will be more disappointed by the
things that you didn't do than by the ones you did do. So
throw off the bowlines. Sail.... Dream. Discover.

—MARK TWAIN

IF I WERE TO WRITE OUT THE DEFINITION OF THE WORD *RIPPLING* AS
I use it, this is how it would go:

Rippling

Throwing a stone into the pool of social change by shaking the
foundations of poverty, inequality, and injustice and spreading
sustainable system change solutions that meet the necessities of
the present by giving those in need the ability to determine their
own future.

By the time you read this chapter you probably don't need a definition; chances are, you've absorbed exactly what *rippling* means, in the true sense of the way I apply it, by experiencing the examples in the book. But if it is going to shake the foundations of poverty, inequality, and injustice, rippling doesn't solely refer to spreading an idea that is powerful enough to spill over borders—it also means "shifting the frame" within which a problem is stuck. It requires going beyond a cause-and-effect approach. It is the theoretical "making lemons out of lemonade," the practical "waking up in the morning and appreciating being alive, rather than grumbling that you'd rather sleep more," or (in the frame-shifting words of Thomas Edison) it is the rational "I have not failed. I have merely found ten thousand ways that won't work."

Just like ocean tides, *rippling* has both a push and a pull quality that encapsulate its ecosystem. It thrusts innovation and cutting-edge thinking outward, and turns it into a source of energy that magnetically pulls changemakers inward, thereby closing the gap between their values, beliefs, circumstances, and goals. Subsequently, that force field of magnetized energy catalyzes collective action and "creates a space where people can find their way into new possibilities."[1] This push-and-pull dynamic and the space created between the nexus of its ebb and flow become part of a newly developed ecosystem that supports Ashoka's "everyone a changemaker" world.

> The image of ripples in a pond provides a simple way to understand the entrepreneurial ecosystem, but it runs the risk of going back to an image of all things in entrepreneurship being about the entrepreneur.... But below the surface of any pond, teeming life forms can be easily missed when focusing only on the surface. Fish, plants, algae, insects, objects, and more all serve a function. And the most distinguishing feature of an ecosystem isn't any one of these things, just as it isn't the pebble or the

person throwing it. It's the interdependence of its community members on one another—for survival, evolution and enhancement. While it may appear that an ecosystem forms or functions to support the needs of one, in reality each member supports the needs and aspirations of the others.[2]

The Outlook Is Partly Sunny

I would also like to define the oft-overused word *change* in the *rippling* sense of the word.

When it comes to the system-changing ideas of the social entrepreneurs in this book, *change* refers to big change, monumental change, change that leaps from household to village, from village to city, from city to country to the world. It means, as my colleague Al Hammond has observed, "To pursue global spread and scale a social entrepreneur must consciously build a supportive ecosystem that is both local and global, can nurture bottom-up and top-down elements of the venture, and can help propagate the idea across national boundaries."[3]

Driving change of this magnitude is not easy to imagine, much less to accomplish. To do this successfully, many people need to be inspired, involved, engaged, and active. All people have the potential to change their own communities for the better—directly by tackling social problems and indirectly by supporting others' ideas. This takes work, time, and persistence on everyone's part. Together, the collective impact is so strong and expansive that it can't be contained by artificially determined geographic borders. It spills out with a one-way flow that cannot be contained. Like Superman, this type of change is more powerful than a locomotive and able to leap tall buildings in a single bound—or more to the point, it's able to leap tall problems in a single solution. (Editorial license exercised!) When societies embrace and promote this belief, a new global system emerges: an "everyone a changemaker" world.[4]

From Common Sense to Common Practice

In the Introduction, I referred to my entrancement with social entrepreneurship when I first discovered Ashoka. In retrospect, after interviewing the eighteen Fellows you have just met in this book, I discovered a number of additional common factors that sustained my respect and increased my admiration.

Micro Intentions, Macro Changes

One and all, these Fellows never thought they would end up doing what they are now doing. They are all amazed at where they are and how they got there. It all originated from their intense compassion to involve themselves in righting an unfair or unequal situation or from their empathy for a repugnant human condition. And it just seemed to grow from there. Since they all think in systems, going beyond cause-and-effect approaches means that there is always one more hurdle to overcome, one more solution to be implanted in the holes in the dyke to restrain human misery. It seems in all these cases that, in the words of William Easterly, "The right plan is to have no plan."[5] However, having a vision is imperative!

The Stickiness of Past Experiences

Each innovation started with a brain click that was turned on by a situation that reminded each of the Fellows of some intimate connection to the problem on which they focused. This relevant connection is what fueled their passion and sustained their persistence. It was as if they did not pick the problem they chose to solve; the problem seemed to pick them by virtue of their past experiences or relationships. For each of the Fellows there was something or someone in their past—something they experienced themselves, someone they knew who was struggling with being differently abled, or something sad or negative that they witnessed years ago—that triggered their involvement. Their need to find solutions represented a situation or encounter that they didn't want others to have to experience again.

Intertwined Identities

When you look at what they have accomplished you realize that in different ways, all eighteen Fellows understand that changemaking comes from the capacity to see the undeveloped potential in every single person, and to support them in discovering their own possibility. They actualize "everyone a changemaker" by truly seeing their community and looking at themselves as an integral part of it. They do not separate themselves from the people they work with. They understand that new voices, visions, and capacities are the products they are developing, and those products will make their community healthier, happier, and more educated, economically stable, and sustainable over the years to come.

Built to Last

Ashoka's social entrepreneurs build institutions around ideas. They understand that impact is not only measured in breadth but in depth as well. They are not so much about how many people they reach; they are mainly concerned with the impact of that reach, the change that ensues, and the sustainability of the system that they leave behind. They have learned that "no individual agent or element determines the nature of a system—the organization of a system arises through the dynamic interaction among the system's agents and through the system's interaction with other systems."[6] Their role is to ignite hope, turn hope into action, and catapult action to impact. To do this they need to let go—to inspire—instead of making all the decisions. They know this element of their program will intensify and strengthen their idea because it will lead to the inclusion and mobilization of multitudes of changemakers.

Turning Culture into Community

Communities are based on people doing their part and investing in their neighbors, and these eighteen social entrepreneurs understand their role in keeping their communities healthy, active, dynamic, and vibrant. They know that poverty is often about economics, and economics is about behavior that is either more or less rational as it responds to its environment.[7] In turn, innovation combined with behavior change has the potential to reshape that same environment. For their solution to be effective, they have all discovered how to get people to act differently in a way that changes not only them but their communities.

The social entrepreneurs in this book are what I would consider positive deviants.[8] It would have been much easier for them to close down their emotions rather than open up to a new and different reality. Life would have become much more predictable, much less threatening, and far simpler if they had just looked straight ahead and stayed on the traditional trail. Once they veered, they often (depending on their location and culture) became anomalies, but their belief in themselves, and in their vision of the way things could be, made them impervious to outside skepticism and worse. One and all, they are, as an Ashoka Fellow once described himself to me, "maybe half crazy, but not stupid."

Accelerating Change Through Technology

Bill Drayton has often said that the key factor for success for any individual, any institution, any country is what percentage of your people are changemakers, and how well they play together both internally and externally.

241

One of the factors that will dramatically enable this interaction to occur will be technology. Social innovation, financial innovation, and disruptive innovation in the twenty-first century will require emerging new tools, new services, new instruments, new mechanisms—not to mention the changing of social practices and behaviors. The computer has changed the protocols around interaction along with expectations of the learning process. And the Web is the architecture that is facilitating and enabling collaborative structures that help move people, teams, and organizations together in various equations over time and space. It is estimated that worldwide there are over 2 billion Internet users (www.internetworldstats.com) and close to 5 billion mobile users (International Telecommunications Union), and it is encouraging to note that of the 800 million Facebook users (Facebook statistic) 125 million are registered in a Facebook cause, signaling how many users are getting involved in social change.

Mobile phones are now imbued with an amazing array of features and are being heralded "as the advance guard for mobile broadband networks that will extend internet access to all."[9] In a world where more people have access to mobile cell phone capabilities than to computers, the ease of mobile messaging and texting—and the advances in e-learning and long distance health care, plus the growth of simple applications and video gaming for social purposes—will allow people to flex their imagination when it comes to creating, designing, and involving themselves in social solutions. Indeed, the world is moving way too fast for anyone to succeed without coordination and collaboration, and the new and emerging technologies are already making that all possible. New technology is unlocking a range of social and economic benefits to users of even the most basic phones—from mobile banking for the unbanked to real-time produce prices for rural farmers to detecting and exposing fraudulent pharmaceuticals and to tracking adherence to tuberculosis and other medical regimens.

On the other end of the social spectrum, technology is also enabling global volunteering on a massive scale—matching people who want to give time helping others but want to do it in the comfort and ease of their own homes. One such online site, Sparked (www.sparked.com), offers convenient online volunteerism for busy professionals who don't have time to lend their expertise to not-for-profits through traditional channels. They make volunteering as much fun, as social, and as easy to use as Facebook, Farmville, or Twitter. Sparked has channeled to charities hundreds of thousands of dollars' worth of skilled professional labor that was previously unavailable to the social sector. It's interactive volunteerism for the digital age, and it has coined a new term for it: microVolunteering.

New and emerging technology is helping to vault social solutions over former geographic, cultural, and socioeconomic barriers. As mentioned in a number of the chapters, social entrepreneurs and a host of changemakers are capitalizing on the use of mobile phones and computers, which in turn will enable a Richter scale shockwave of measurable change that eventually extends to the bottom of the world's deepest economic crater.

The Vitality of the Virtuous Cycle: From Margins to Mainstream

Most innovations start small, as part of the citizen or the business sector. In the United States, small businesses are said to be the backbone of the economy as they are responsible for employing more than half of all employable people. Similar statistics exist for most developed and developing countries around the world. And the citizen sector is no wallflower when it comes to the comparative numbers of people it employs. Indeed, the largest employer in Bangladesh (the poorest country in the southern hemisphere) is BRAC, now a global nonprofit organization that employs more than ninety thousand people in Bangladesh alone. Because social entrepreneurs know that scale is not based on numbers alone but on how those numbers will impact the world, their organizational structures make it possible for changemakers to move ideas through society to get hundreds of people from every continent to spread their solutions. Inherently, their institutions create a cycle of hiring and employment, anywhere from one to ninety thousand, that in today's world should be recognized as a jobs creation contribution as important as small business's (which in essence many of these organizations could be considered).

As they co-create and grow these organizations with the communities that benefit from them, they are constantly training changemakers, who are consistently developing new skills. They increase employment opportunities by involving community and corporate partners in the effort. They create sustainable jobs that in turn cascade into employment opportunities for people at all levels of the capabilities spectrum. The more effectively they scale, the more they increase their ability to employ huge numbers of changemakers—and those agents of change, in turn, employ others. The potential of the citizen sector to effect employment as a secondary consequence of its solution-development focus is, in the middle of today's world economy, especially worthy of attention. Indeed, "The social economy is the next new economy."[10]

Then; Now; From Now On

When I resigned from the job I alluded to in the Introduction to join Ashoka, my perceptive former boss said to me, "If I thought you were leaving because of time or money, I would try to rectify the situation—but I know you are leaving for heart, and there is nothing I can offer you to have you stay. You need to follow your heart." Her words capsulated the long process of introspection that had led to my resignation. I realized that I had felt I had so many commitments—to my job, to my ailing parents, to my daily life and lifestyle—that I couldn't distinguish those from what was most meaningful and significant to me, nor could I separate them from the type of life I wanted to build for myself. When I finally decided to take the time to reflect deeply, I asked myself what was the only thing standing between me and fulfilling my desire to support social change in the world. It came down to fear of jumping off the high board into a strange pool and being afraid that I would have forgotten how to swim. So the action I decided to take was to jump in heart first—and that seemed to conquer my excuses, my indecisiveness and my fear of drowning. As Joseph Campbell once said,

"We must let go of the life we have planned so as to accept the one that is waiting for us."

Not Either Or, But Both and More[11]

In 2011, French diplomat, ambassador, concentration camp survivor, and French Resistance fighter Stephane Hessel published the English-language edition of a book called *Indignez-Vous!* (Time for Outrage). "This is what I tell young people," he says. "If you spend a little time searching, you will find your reasons to engage. The worst attitude is indifference.[12] If you look closely (and maybe not so closely), I'm sure you will find plenty of reasons to engage wherever you live. For at one time or another haven't most of us thought it shameful that there are people living on the streets, or been outraged about violence in our neighborhood, or annoyed with a less-than-acceptable school system, or furious with a nonresponsive public program that we had counted on for help? If you've thought it disgracefully shameful that children in many countries are dying by the thousands of preventable diseases for lack of vaccines and medication; if you've heard yourself saying, "Why doesn't someone do something to fix this?" then instead, ask yourself if *you* just might be that someone who could help. Think about the people in this book who used to be just like you: a housewife, a corporate banker, a journalist, a teacher, a veterinarian, a social worker, a security guard, a widow, a PhD microbiologist, a truck driver, an activist, a computer systems expert. Everyone in the book started by changing the ways things were—on the ground around them. You don't have to become a social entrepreneur and build your own solution; even trying to find out more about the issues—so your annoyance is fully informed—is a move in the right direction.

Ask yourself, if you were starting out all over again in your career or life path, how would you reframe yourself? Where would you find fulfillment? What would you redo or re-create, and why are you feeling that it is too late to do it now? Feel free to use this book as a permission slip to begin the introspective process and envision how you fit into the social iconography. Give yourself permission to see the opportunities and instead of saying it's *im*possible, say, "*I'm* possible." Channel your annoyance, your indignation, your outrage, your empathy, your sense of sadness into a positive action.

The way people imagine society affects what they do and how they perceive everyday occurrences. The value of what you see depends on how you see it. It is difficult to make a better future until you can imagine one, so imagine yourself creating the future you want to see in the world. Unless you can envision an alternative future for yourself, your family, your community, and the world, we will never have one.

Social entrepreneurship is all about bringing new opportunities into the arena of solutions and sponsoring a process that will enable new people and voices to participate in the emerging system being created. Maybe you are just that new opportunity—and maybe, if you are not already there, you will soon find your way into the arena. Maybe this book will help get you there.

Most people don't know there are angels whose only job is to make sure you don't get too comfortable and fall asleep and miss your life.

—BRIAN ANDREAS, *STORYPEOPLE*

How to Think About Tomorrow

I WAS ENCOURAGED BY MANY PEOPLE TO MAKE THE LAST PAGE IN the book "a call to action" so readers who were intrigued, interested, and inspired by an "everyone a changemaker" world would put down this book and immediately become part of it. It felt pretentious for me to give you a prescription for how to get more involved in your own life. But a colleague of mine recently shared some reflections that she and a friend developed while attending a Singularity University (www.singularityu.org) program. I really found them meaningful, and for all of you who are contemplating jumping off the high board into the pool of social change, I hope this mix of advice and actions bring you closer to the water.[1]

Lessons on Social Entrepreneurship

Take Responsibility for Your Life
Transform your mind-set from waiting for other people to approve, agree, or judge the worth of your ideas to staying in the driver's seat

and taking other people's reactions and ideas as input for further iterations of your ideas. To do this:

1. Put your ideas and self out there.
2. Observe how others respond.
3. Use their feedback to analyze and improve upon your idea, but do not take the feedback personally or let others label your idea as good or bad or right or wrong.
4. Once you have incorporated the feedback in a way that you are comfortable with, share the idea again.
5. Keep repeating the process until the actions you need to take are clarified in your own mind.

Stay Objective

Your first job is to prove the worth of your idea to yourself by examining all possibilities rather than proving the worth of your idea to someone else.

Once you have done that work, everyone else will be convinced.

1. Learn to observe before taking sides or forming conclusions.
2. Take time to observe the big picture. You will be successful if you can implement a strategy that is a win-win situation for all. If you do this, your work will be a series of pieces magically falling together rather than a situation where it is a fight every step of the way.
3. Respect others and see yourself as an equal with others (not below, not above). No matter who it is. Changemaking involves empowering others as equals and working for everyone to reach their highest potential.
4. After careful analysis and observation, stand up for the good; in an entrepreneurial world where all is equal, it is what lasts.

Act

If there is something you want to do, then do it. We live in a chaotic world, and acting creates advantages as it opens up possibilities.

1. Start at the top, working with the best people you can find.
2. Be comfortable with not knowing the outcome.
3. Keep things moving.
4. Have a "nothing is impossible" attitude; aspire to the highest level change you are willing to tackle.

Problems

1. Don't have them. Only have solutions.

Author's Note

In the 2007 movie *The Bucket List*, while looking at the ancient pyramids at Giza, Morgan Freeman turns to Jack Nicholson and remarks, "You know, the ancient Egyptians had a beautiful belief about death. When their souls got to the entrance to heaven, the guards asked two questions. 'Have you found joy in your life?' 'Has your life brought joy to others?'" Their answers determined whether the souls were able to enter or not.

Enough said. I hope that I, along with everyone in this book, have brought joy to your life, and you will be ready and able to pass that joy onto others.

And let me know how you're doing. Please visit www .changemakers.com/Rippling.

NOTES

Prologue

1. "Boy on a High Dive" was the cover of the August 16, 1947, issue of the *Saturday Evening Post*. See, for example, www.nrm.org/2010/01/e-newsletter-quiz/attachment/031/; viewed September 28, 2011.

Introduction

1. Allen L. White, "The Future of the Corporation," *Leading Perspectives*, Business for Social Responsibility, Fall 2005, p. 5; available online at www.bsr.org/reports/leading-perspectives/2005/2005-fall .pdf; viewed October 1, 2011.

2. Beverly Schwartz, "The Freedom to Innovate: The Contributions of Social Entrepreneurs to the Field of Global Public Health," in Paul A. Gaist (ed.), *Igniting the Power of Community: The Role of CBOs and NGOs in Global Public Health* (New York: Springer, 2010), p. 81.

3. Schwartz, "Freedom to Innovate," p. 81.

4. David Bornstein, *How to Change the World: Social Entrepreneurs and the Power of New Ideas* (New York: Oxford University Press, 2004); David Bornstein and Susan Davis, *Social Entrepreneurship: What Everyone Needs to Know* (New York: Oxford University Press, 2010); John Elkington and Pamela Hartigan, *The Power of*

251

Unreasonable People: How Social Entrepreneurs Create Markets That Change the World (Boston: Harvard Business Press, 2008).

Chapter 1

1. Unless otherwise noted all quotations and figures are taken from personal interviews, from the profiles created when the social entrepreneurs were elected to the Ashoka Fellowship, or from their websites, annual reports, and the like. All interviews were conducted by the author except for three conducted and translated by Ashoka staff, as mentioned in the acknowledgments.
2. Jürgen Reuss, "Peaceful Rebels: How a Small Town in the Black Forest Opted Out of Nuclear Power," *Atlantic Times*, November 2008; available online: www.atlantic-times.com/archive_detail.php?recordID=1538; viewed September 2, 2011.

Chapter 5

1. David Bornstein, *The Price of a Dream: The Story of the Grameen Bank and the Idea That Is Helping the Poor Change Their Lives* (New York: Simon & Schuster, 1996).
2. Greg Van Kirk, "The MicroConsignment Model: Bridging the 'Last Mile' of Access to Products and Services for the Rural Poor," *Innovations*, Special Edition, Tech4society, MIT Press, 2010, p. 145; available online at http://tech.ashoka.org/sites/tech/files/INNOVATIONS_Invention_Led_Development_Van_Kirk.pdf; viewed October 1, 2011.

Chapter 6

1. Gretchen Wilson, "Kenya's Farmers Connect to Better Prices," American Public Media Marketplace, February 19, 2007; available online: http://marketplace.publicradio.org/display/web/2007/02/19/kenyas_farmers_connect_to_better_prices/; viewed September 28, 2011.

Chapter 10

1. Re the estimate of 2.6 billion people without access to toilet facilities, see "World's Toilet Crisis," Adam Yamaguichi, Correspondent/Executive Producer, Current TV, originally aired June 9, 2010; available online: http://current.com/shows/vanguard/episodes/season-four/worlds-toilet-crisis/; viewed September 3, 2011.

Chapter 12

1. "Better World Entrepreneurs: How a Force, No Matter How Small, Can Impact Change and Betterment of Global Societies," *Bangkok Post*, August 16, 2008.
2. "FNB Namibia Launches Support of Aflatoun," FNB Namibia, August 11, 2010; available online: www.fnbnamibia.com.na/news/archive/2010/20100811Support.html; viewed October 17, 2011.

Chapter 13

1. Stefan Wilhelm, "Intelligent Optimists: Dr. Andreas Heinecke," odemagazine.com, August 20, 2009; available online: www.odemagazine.com/blogs/intelligent_optimists/9303/dr_andreas_heinecke; viewed September 28, 2011.
2. Dialogue Social Enterprise, Annual Report 2010, p. 87.

Chapter 14

1. Susan Donovan, "Entrepreneur Thorkil Sonne on What You Can Learn from Employees with Autism," *Harvard Business Review*, September 2008; available online: http://hbr.org/2008/09/entrepreneur-thorkil-sonne-on-what-you-can-learn-from-employees-with-autism/ar/1; viewed September 8, 2011.

Chapter 15

1. Paul Scheltus, "Argentina's 'Loony Radio' Threatened by Hospital Closure," *Independent*, June 11, 2008; available online:

www.independent.co.uk/news/world/americas/argentinas-loony-radio-threatened-by-hospital-closure-844166.html; viewed September 16, 2011.

2. Find *Tetro* at www.amazon.com/s/ref=nb_sb_noss?url=search-alias%3Dmovies-tv&field-keywords=coppola+tetro&x=0&y=0 and "Radio La Colifata Presenta: El Canto Del Loco" CD/DVD at www.amazon.com/Radio-Colifata-Presenta-Canto-Loco/dp/B002ZDOXQM. The album "Viva La Colifata with Manu Chao" is available for free download at www.vivalacolifata.org/.

Chapter 17

1. For the history of Yunus and the Grameen Bank, see David Bornstein, *The Price of a Dream: The Story of the Grameen Bank and the Idea That Is Helping the Poor Change Their Lives* (New York: Simon & Schuster, 1996).

2. Laurie Goodstein, "An Effort to Foster Tolerance in Religion," *New York Times*, June 13, 2011; available online: www.nytimes.com/2011/06/14/us/14patel.html?_r=1&ref=lauriegoodstein; viewed August 26, 2011.

3. *This American Moment*, NPR, October 2, 2008.

4. Joshua Stanton is founding co-editor of *the Journal of Inter-Religious Dialogue*. The *Journal of Inter-Religious Dialogue* can be found at www.irdialogue.org, with a subsidiary (and less academic) website for emerging religious leaders at www.stateofformation.org.

Conclusion

1. "Forces for Social Change and Civic Renewal," Harwood Institute Report, December 2008, p. 110.

2. Larry Robertson, *A Deliberate Pause: Entrepreneurship and Its Moment in Human Progress* (New York: Morgan James, 2009), p. 93.

3. Allen Hammond, "BoP Venture Formation for Scale," in *Next-Generation Business Strategies for the Base of the Pyramid: New*

Approaches for Building Mutual Value, edited by T. London and
S. L. Hart (Upper Saddle River, NJ: Financial Times Press, 2010),
pp. 193–216.

4. Ashoka Fellows Changing Systems, Global Study 2009, p. 21.

5. William Easterly, *The White Man's Burden: Why the West's Efforts to Aid the Rest Have Done So Much Ill and So Little Good* (New York: Penguin, 2006), p. 5.

6. WHO and Alliance for Health Policy and Systems Research Report, "Systems Thinking for Health Systems Strengthening," 2009, p. 40.

7. Esther Duflo, quoted in Ian Parker, "The Poverty Lab," *New Yorker*, May 17, 2010, pp. 79–89.

8. Richard Pascale, Jerry Sternin, and Monique Sternin, *The Power of Positive Deviance: How Unlikely Innovators Solve the World's Toughest Problems* (Boston: Harvard Business Press, 2010).

9. *The Economist*, Special Report: "Telecoms in Emerging Markets: Mobile Marvels." September 24, 2009; available online: www.economist.com/node/14483896; viewed September 27, 2011.

10. Outlook Business, "Editor's Note: Think About It," September 5, 2009, p. 1; available online: http://business.outlookindia.com/article.aspx?261363; viewed October 20, 2011.

11. The heading acknowledges the title of a forthcoming book by Dr. Ralph Wittenberg.

12. Stephane Hessel, *A Time For Outrage*, North American Edition (New York: Hachette, 2011), p. 11.

Epilogue

1. Thanks to Darlene Damm and Diego Favarolo for the lessons on social entrepreneurship.

ACKNOWLEDGMENTS

A GOOD FRIEND OF MINE IS CONVINCED THAT WHENEVER I NEED something, someone always seems to magically appear and provide me with a piece of information or an offering that would help me out. When it came to the writing of this book, I have to agree with her. Many people magically appeared to make this possible. First and foremost my friend and colleague Maria Clara Pinhiero (the origin of the statement just noted), who from the moment I described the book project has done just about everything possible to make sure I finished it, including conducting the interviews for Chapter Seven in Portuguese and translating them into English. And my other friends and colleagues Iman Bibars, Chimney Chetty, and Ewa Konzcal, who nudged me along when I needed pushing, and Paula Cardenau and Simon Stumpf, who conducted interviews in both Spanish and English to make it possible for me to include two Fellows with whom I could not have communicated otherwise.

Along the way, my friends in Washington D.C., notably Ruth Marcus, Jerry Malitz and Gregory Niblett, provided me with food, fun, friendship, and much advice to break up the long stretches of quiet contemplation and writing, while my caring and supportive friends across the country and the world provided similar comfort, either in person or via phone or Internet. A double thanks to friends Patrice and Kip Jones, who lent me a place to write when I needed solitude, and to Paul Gaist, who reminded me how much I enjoy writing (and how much I have to say) when he asked me to submit a chapter for his book, *Igniting the Power of Community*.

Thanks to Bill Drayton, who gave me the inspiration, space, time, and encouragement I needed, to all the Ashoka staff, past and present, and to the Ashoka Fellows who have helped shape my thinking and contributed in ways big and small (you know who you are). A special thank-you for the eighteen Fellows in the book, who shared their time and their personal stories with me, and to Susan Mieselas and the Magnum Foundation staff, who helped pilot the dream of a visual project to accompany the book that we still hope to fulfill. And to sister Linda, my niece Sarin, and my nephew Bryson, who shared my excitement throughout the process.

The five approaches to system change representing the five sections of the book are based on "Ashoka Fellows Changing Systems Survey," 2009, conducted by Karabi Acharya, which in turn, was inspired by previous studies by Ashoka's president Diana Wells. The survey and the time they spent discussing the results were immensely helpful in framing my thinking. And lastly, a special nod to Jesse Wiley (Jossey-Bass/Wiley), who opened the first door and made the book a reality.

If you are taking the time to read this page, there is a good chance that you have probably helped make the book possible and thought that your name might have been mentioned here. If it's not, I apologize—but please know that I appreciated any and all of the help, support, nurturing, and encouragement that you sent my way.

ABOUT THE AUTHOR

BEVERLY SCHWARTZ IS AN ENTREPRENEURIAL BEHAVIORAL SCIENTIST and social marketing expert skilled in creating social change through policy advocacy and the management of large-scale marketing, communications, media, and advertising programs for the profit, public, and citizen sectors. She is a veteran of managing expansive social marketing campaigns, and as such, she has devoted her career to working on some of the world's most challenging health and educational issues encompassing both domestic and global perspectives. Her portfolio includes topics as diverse as smoking prevention and nonsmokers' rights for the Minnesota Lung Association, the National Council on Smoking and Health and the U.S. Centers for Disease Control and Prevention; eye care and the prevention of sight loss for the American Academy of Ophthalmology; drug prevention for Fleishman-Hillard Communications and the National Youth Anti-Drug Media campaign under the auspices of the Executive Office of the White House; gender equity in education for the World Bank and the U.S. Agency for International Development; education and environmental reform for the Academy for Educational Development (AED, now FHI360);

and HIV/AIDS awareness and prevention for the U.S. Centers for Disease Control and Prevention as one of the key creators and managers of its "America Responds to AIDS" campaign in the critical growth years between 1987 and 1992. In the three years (between 1972 and 1975) that Beverly lived in Minnesota, she helped write and pass the Minnesota Clean Indoor Air Act, the nation's first nonsmoking in public places state law.

For the past seven years, Beverly has been vice president of global marketing for Ashoka, the world's largest association of leading social entrepreneurs. Her present behavioral challenge is to empower all people, everywhere, to be positive forces for change in the world.

She holds a BA degree in education and an MS degree from the City University of New York, Queens College. A native of New York City, she has lived in Minneapolis, San Francisco, and Atlanta, and currently resides in Washington D.C.

Beverly is a member of the Board of Trustees of the National Hospice Foundation. She is an avid scuba diver and her most consistent companion when traveling internationally is her dive gear.

About Ashoka

Ashoka (www.ashoka.org) is the global association of the world's leading social entrepreneurs—men and women with system-changing solutions for the world's most urgent social problems. There are currently over 3,000 Ashoka Fellows around the globe. Ashoka is non–sector specific and helps ensure the success of any entity, region, or field by finding the best new ideas, by cultivating the changemaker talent to act on those ideas, and by developing new collaborations and designing entrepreneurial programs that encourage and allow major change to happen.

As Ashoka expands its capacity to integrate and connect social and business entrepreneurs around the world, it builds an entrepreneurial infrastructure comprised of global initiatives that supports the ever evolving and fast-growing needs of tomorrow. Ashoka is helping create change today, for an "everyone a changemaker" society to become the reality of tomorrow.

INDEX